THE BATTLE OF FREDERICKSBURG

THE BATTLE OF FREDERICKSBURG

WE CANNOT ESCAPE HISTORY

JAMES K. BRYANT II

Series Editor Doug Bostick

THE
History
PRESS

www.historypress.net

Cover image: *In the Hands of Providence* by Mort Küntsler. © 2003 Mort Küntsler, Inc.
www.mkuntsler.com.

First published 2010
Second printing 2012

ISBN 978.1.5402.2091.2

Bryant, James K.
The Battle of Fredericksburg : we cannot escape history / James K. Bryant II.
p. cm.
Includes bibliographical references.
ISBN 978-1-5402-2091-2
1. Fredericksburg, Battle of, Fredericksburg, Va., 1862. I. Title.
E474.85.B86 2010
973.7'33--dc22
2010020768

Contents

Introduction

A Good Friday

The date was April 18, 1862, and it was Good Friday when Federal forces occupied Falmouth, Virginia, in Stafford County across the Rappahannock River from Fredericksburg. Nine days later, longtime Fredericksburg resident Jane Briggs Howison Beale recorded in her diary:

> *Fredericksburg is a captured town, the enemy took possession of the Stafford hills…and their guns have frowned down upon us ever since, fortunately for us our troops were enabled to burn the bridges connecting our town with the Stafford shore and thus saved us the presence of the Northern soldiers in our midst, but our releif* [sic] *from this annoyance will not be long as they have brought boats to the wharf and will of course be enabled to cross at their pleasure, it is painfully humiliating to feel one's self* [sic] *a captive, but all sorrow for self is now lost in the deeper feeling of anxiety for our army, for our cause, we have lost every thing* [sic]*, regained nothing, our army has fallen back before the superior forces of the enemy until but a small strip of our Old Dominion is left to us, our sons are all in the field and we who are now in the hands of the enemy cannot even hear from them, must their precious young lives be sacrificed, their homes made desolate, our cause be lost and all our rights be trampled under foot of a vindictive foe, Gracious God avert from us these terrible calamities! Rise in thy Majesty and strength and rebuke our enemies.*

Above: A sketch of McDowell's troops entering Fredericksburg on May 5, 1862. This would be the first major period of "enemy" occupation of the town during the war. One resident prayed: "Gracious God avert from us these terrible calamities!" *Forbes, Library of Congress.*

Left: Major General Irvin McDowell (1818–1885), the head of Federal forces at their defeat at First Bull Run (First Manassas) in June 1861, commanded the Department of the Rappahannock from April 4 to June 26, 1862. He proclaimed Fredericksburg "a position of Manifest importance to us and to the enemy." *Library of Congress.*

8

A Good Friday

Confederate sergeant John Hampden Chamberlayne of the Purcell (Virginia) Artillery wrote to his mother: "The evacuation of Fredericksburg went to my heart, it…is one of the few places, one of the last abodes where lingers the old time spirit of Virginia gentry, their quiet high breeding & elegant refinement of feeling & manner. To me at least the town seems one of the most precious places we had." Ham Chamberlayne would return to Fredericksburg later that December, participating in some of the most horrific fighting experienced in the war to date.

It would not be until May 2 that Federal troops began a period of occupation of Fredericksburg proper. These troops, as part of the recently organized Department of the Rappahannock under the overall command of Major General Irvin McDowell, would continue to cause tension among Fredericksburg's residents.

McDowell called Fredericksburg "a position of Manifest importance to us and to the enemy, whatever course the war may take."[1] His troops would serve as strategic reinforcements for Federal operations in Virginia. Fredericksburg became a central communications network, a major supply base and route of transportation to quickly aid the Army of the Potomac under Major General George McClellan attempting to capture the Confederate capital at Richmond to the southeast or assist Federal forces under Major General Nathaniel P. Banks to the northwest in the Shenandoah Valley fighting Confederate forces under Major General Thomas J. "Stonewall" Jackson.

Federal forces remained in Fredericksburg until August 31 in the aftermath of the defeat of Major General John Pope's Army of Virginia by General Robert E. Lee and the Confederate Army of Northern Virginia at the Battle of Second Bull Run (Second Manassas). Mrs. Beale's "annoyance" over the presence of Federal soldiers would be magnified four months later when Fredericksburg was occupied once again by Federal soldiers. This time, Fredericksburg would be the center of a major military campaign.

The Battle of Fredericksburg is known as the most disastrous defeat the Federal Army of the Potomac experienced in the American Civil War. The futile assaults by Federal soldiers against the Confederate defensive positions on Marye's Heights and behind the infamous stone wall along the "Sunken Road" solidified Ambrose Burnside's reputation as an inept army commander and reinforced Robert E. Lee's undefeatable image. Two decades after Fredericksburg, Francis W. Palfrey, an Army of the Potomac veteran, made some observations of his former command in the campaign study *The Antietam and Fredericksburg*. He wrote:

Fredericksburg, Virginia, viewed from the eastern bank of the Rappahannock River in November 1862. The town, situated halfway between the two warring capitals of Washington, D.C., and Richmond, Virginia, had 5,022 residents before the war. *Library of Congress.*

It would be too much to say that there are no sadder stories in military history than that of the Army of the Potomac, but its story is sad enough. Always better than its commanders, always ready to "stand in the evil hour," and "having done all to stand," it marched and fought and hungered and thirsted for four long years, hardly ever animated by victory. It showed in all that it endured and achieved, that it was an admirable instrument for the hand that knew how to wield it, but it never had the good fortune to be commanded by a soldier who was worthy of it. It fought through to the end, it did its work and gained its crown, but its path was long and rough and seldom cheered, and one of its saddest and sharpest experiences was its brave, hopeless effort at Fredericksburg [2]

Postwar reminiscences of participants on both sides at Fredericksburg often sought to highlight and defend their own actions or correct what was perceived as historical inaccuracies through numerous memoirs and regimental histories. In 1884, *Century* magazine compiled the *Battles and Leaders of the Civil War* series with its third volume, devoting a chapter titled "Burnside at Fredericksburg." Numerous articles written by former Federals and Confederates provided the basis for the historical interpretation of Fredericksburg that continued to prevail for much of the twentieth century. [3]

Edward J. Stackpole's *Drama on the Rappahannock: The Fredericksburg Campaign* (1957) served as one of the first attempts at a modern comprehensive narrative on the subject. Fredericksburg became the central feature of Federal operations on the Rappahannock River:

> *Notwithstanding its valued colonial heritage, it was not until December 1862 that Fredericksburg, with a population of only four thousand, attained the distinction of being one of a comparatively small number of Americans cities or towns whose names are synonymous with famous battles. During the Civil War it changed hands seven times, was fiercely fought over in the campaigns of Fredericksburg and Chancellorsville, and by the close of the war had dwindled to two thousand souls.*

Nevertheless, Stackpole still perpetuated the traditional interpretation of Fredericksburg without placing it into the broader context of the war.[4]

Fortunately, George C. Rable's *Fredericksburg! Fredericksburg!* (2002) and Francis A. O'Reilly's *The Fredericksburg Campaign: Winter War on the Rappahannock* (2003) have been two book-length narratives and long overdue treatments of the Fredericksburg Campaign within the past fifty-two years. Although complementing each other, both works approach Fredericksburg from different perspectives, lifting it from the depths of irrelevancy in the annals of Civil War history.[5]

Rable views Fredericksburg not from just traditional military history—emphasizing leaders and battle plans—but also focuses on the lives of common soldiers and their connections to larger social themes of the middle period of American history:

> *In many ways Fredericksburg had woven together the mundane, the horrific, and the transcendent. Everyday matters such as shelter, clothing, food, pay, and letters had loomed larger for the common soldiers than campaigns or strategies. Yet generals' plans along with privates' fears and junior officers' ambitions had influences the pace and texture of military life. Bloody combat occurred in the context of family news, politics, ideology, religion, and rumor. It tore at emotions, often undermining or solidifying faith in leadership and the respective causes.*

O'Reilly's impeccable and intimate knowledge of the Fredericksburg Battlefield places it in a prominent role in the evolution of military science and its influence, as well as impact, on the politics of the day when compared to the other "landmark" Civil War campaigns. Additionally, he offers fresh interpretation of the battle itself with his emphasis that the fighting on the southern end of the battlefield at Hamilton's Crossing and Prospect Hill was the decisive point of action instead of the often remembered slaughter of Federal troops in front of the stone wall below Marye's Heights. O'Reilly provides a glimpse of the political implications of Fredericksburg when he writes:

> *The Civil War entered a unique, new phase in the fall of 1862. Lincoln's need for victory demanded an unprecedented winter campaign...The Union armies started their campaigns ill prepared and poorly equipped to handle a winter expedition for some tenuous political capital by his largest and most newsworthy army, Burnside's Army of the Potomac.*[6]

Fredericksburg emerges as an explicit example of the relationship between politics and war as espoused by early nineteenth-century military theorist Carl von Clausewitz. "War is nothing but a continuation of political intercourse," he maintained. As such, war was a means to achieve political ends. By mid-1862, President Abraham Lincoln began steering the United States toward the emancipation of slaves as part of the Union war effort. This could not be achieved until Federal armies could enforce such policies in the Southern slave states in which the citizens were in a state of rebellion. If the Battle of Antietam offered the occasion for the issuance of Lincoln's Preliminary Emancipation Proclamation of September 22, 1862, the Battle of Fredericksburg would be the decisive contest to restore the Union with emancipation as the means achieving this result.[7]

Robert E. Lee and the Army of Northern Virginia, as the military agents of the Confederate States of America, held the means to achieve the political ends of Jefferson Davis on a smaller and more immediate scale than their Northern counterparts. Maintaining morale and support among the civilian populace in the Confederacy was as important as doing so with the military. The Army of the Potomac's advance toward Richmond in November 1862 forced Lee's Confederates to assume a defensive posture in protecting the Confederate capital at Richmond. Although preferring to make a stout defense in positions closer to Richmond than at Fredericksburg, Lee deliberately chose Fredericksburg to make his stand against Burnside for political considerations.

Fredericksburg not only became a key military terrain feature for both sides but also suffered from the hard fortunes of war as did its residents, both permanent and transients. The fateful month of December 1862 proved to be the low point for the Army of the Potomac and perhaps the Union war

A 1920 photograph of what was likely a slave auction block on the corner of William and Charles Streets in Fredericksburg, Virginia. Although slavery ended fifty-five years before, former Fredericksburg slave John M. Washington recalled with sorrow witnessing slaves "with little Bundles strapped to their backs, men, women, and children…and all marched off to be Sold South away from all that was near and dear to them." *Library of Congress.*

effort but a significant high point for the Confederacy. Could the Union war effort sustain emancipation as a viable war aim in a risky and unprecedented winter campaign?

A byproduct of Federal occupation in the Fredericksburg area was the influx of fugitive slaves seeking refuge within Federal-held lines. This had begun with the occupation in April 1862. Mrs. Beale complained in her journal on May 14 concerning the effect that the enemy soldiers had on the slaves in the local community:

> [T]*he enemy has interfered with our labour by inducing servants* [slaves] *to leave us and many families are left without the help they have been accustomed to in their domestic arrangements. They tell the servants not to leave, but to demand wages. this policy may suit them very well as it will prevent the north from feeling the great evil of a useless, expensive*

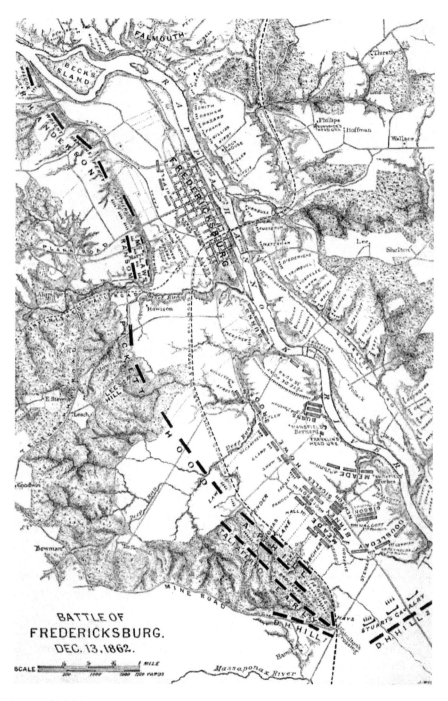

A map of initial troop positions at the Battle of Fredericksburg on December 13, 1862. *Battles and Leaders of the Civil War, vol. 3.*

and degraded population among them, but it strikes at the root of those principles and rights for which our Southern people are contending and cannot be submitted to, it fixes upon us this incubus of supporting a race, who were ordained of high Heaven to serve the white man and it is only in that capacity they can be happy useful and respected.

It seemed that the loss of slaves affected her neighbors more than it did her. Professing her love for her slaves as she did her own children, Beale hoped to maintain their happiness without placing herself and her slaves "in a more unhappy position than that which we now occupy" under the evil influences of Federal soldiers.

John M. Washington, a young slave residing in Fredericksburg, held a different view when McDowell's men first occupied Falmouth on April 18, 1862:

Every man servant was out on the house top looking over the River at the Yankees for their glistening bayonets could Easily be seen I could not begin to Express my new born hopes for I felt already like I was certain of My freedom Now.[8]

For Washington and countless numbers of slaves, Fredericksburg would become a flagship to freedom. The date April 18, 1862, would indeed prove to be a Good Friday.

Chapter 1

I Shall Not Surrender This Game

Lincoln and Emancipation Politics

Fredericksburg was Abraham Lincoln's battle. It was his battle to win or lose as he attempted to achieve his ultimate war aim of preserving the Union. By the midsummer of 1862, emancipation had become a key component to this war aim. "I claim not to have controlled events," Lincoln wrote to a Kentucky newspaper editor, "but confess plainly that events have controlled me."[9] It would be the flurry of events unleashed by war that would bring Lincoln to the realization that he had to make direct and definitive policy ending slavery, and Fredericksburg figured in the process.

Lincoln had long defined himself as possessing antislavery principles, believing the "peculiar institution" a detriment to the national progress, and hoped that it would become extinct over time. After the first shots of the Civil War were exchanged at Fort Sumter, South Carolina, on April 12, 1861, Lincoln's policy of preserving the Union was top priority. Slavery would be maintained where it existed in the remaining loyal slave states ("border states"). Some Federal military commanders in these particular states generally enforced the Fugitive Slave Act of 1850, which required the return of runaway slaves to owners who petitioned for their return and who claimed loyalty to the United States. However, not all Federal commanders acted in unison. Those possessing abolitionist tendencies believed that the war presented opportunities for full emancipation of slaves. Lincoln, forced to demonstrate his early commitment of not making emancipation a part of his policies, reversed such decisions of his generals on at least two occasions.

In August 1861, Major General John C. Frémont, commanding Federal forces in Missouri, declared martial law for the entire state, emancipating all slaves owned by citizens taking up arms against the United States. Fearful of losing Missouri to the Confederacy, Lincoln revoked Frémont's order, concluding that the general's actions "will alarm our Southern Union friends and turn them against us."

Similarly in May 1862, Major General David Hunter—commanding Federal forces occupying the coastal areas of South Carolina, Georgia and Florida and declaring "[s]lavery and martial law in a free country are altogether incompatible"—ordered the emancipation of slaves in these states. Lincoln rescinded Hunter's order,

Abraham Lincoln (1809–1865), the sixteenth president of the United States, had the monumental task of holding the nation together. He needed the Army of the Potomac, the premier Federal army in the eastern theatre, to bring him much-needed victories for his fledgling political fortunes in 1862. *Library of Congress.*

noting that such questions he reserved for himself as commander in chief and that he "cannot feel justified in leaving to the decision of commanders in the field."[10] Lincoln could not afford to lose Missouri, Kentucky and Maryland, states with divided loyalties. Moreover, he deemed it crucial to maintain property rights, including slaves, in areas of the South under Federal control.

The first test of "controlling events" had come in the form of three fugitive slaves seeking refuge at Union-held Fort Monroe, Virginia. Major General Benjamin F. Butler, a Massachusetts Democrat, commanded the fort and presented the earliest government policy concerning fugitive slaves in May 1861, declaring fugitive slaves employed in the construction of Confederate artillery batteries arrayed against the fort at nearby Hampton as "contrabands of war" duly captured and confiscated from the enemy. Influenced by Butler's actions, the U.S. Congress passed a Confiscation Act on August 6, 1861, declaring that slave owners in open insurrection against the United States forfeited their claim to ownership (and implying slave confiscation by the government) but not giving slaves the status of freedmen. The status of confiscated slaves was the particular aspect that got Frémont into trouble with Lincoln a little over three weeks after the passage of this act.[11]

The growing presence and use of fugitive slaves by military authorities in Federal-occupied areas of the South prompted the U.S. Congress, yet again, to pass a series of bills on July 17, 1862, that not only freed all slaves captured by Federal forces or slaves of disloyal owners escaping on their own accord but also allowed for the enrollment of suitable persons of "African descent" into the military "under such regulations, not inconsistent with the Constitution and laws, as the President may prescribe."[12]

On the surface, Congress, dominated by Republicans with the absence of Southern representatives, seemed to be at cross purposes with the Republican Lincoln in bringing emancipation to the forefront of Union war aims. But all Republican lawmakers and governmental officials did not think alike. The exclusion of slavery in U.S. territories, as well as in future states, and staunch support for the war effort against the rebellion were their unifying issues. Republican ideology ranged from individuals proclaiming abstract antislavery principles on political and economic ground that did not espouse equality for African Americans to those who sought equality for all Americans regardless of race. Republicans even differed on the process of emancipation itself. Those considered conservative or moderate Republicans, if they did not support a restructuring of Southern society, tended to seek gradual emancipation of slaves, with some, especially Lincoln, supporting compensation to loyal owners for the loss of their chattel property. Radical Republicans tended to lean toward immediate emancipation and a complete overhaul of the Southern landscape once the war concluded. Complicating matters for Lincoln was the creation of the Joint Committee on the Conduct of the War at the end of 1861. Composed of members of both houses of Congress and having a Republican majority, the committee investigated a range of military matters, ultimately promoting the Radical Republican agenda that Lincoln had been unwilling to follow this early in the war. The committee's existence not only demonstrated the different factions within the Republican Party but also posed potential conflict between the executive and legislative branches of government in the overall prosecution of the war.[13]

In response to the emancipation of slaves in Washington, D.C., in April 1862, Lincoln sent a message to both houses of Congress. "I am gratified that the two principles of compensation, and colonization, are both recognized, and practically applied in the act," he wrote.[14] Compensated emancipation had been formulating in Lincoln's mind as early as November 1861, when he composed two drafts of a gradual emancipation plan using the border state of Delaware as a test case. The state was the smallest of any of the slave states and seemingly stood the least to lose if its slaves were emancipated. Similar support from other border states might compel the rebellious states in the South to adopt his proposal. In his annual message to Congress the following month, Lincoln had recommended legislation that not only encouraged cooperation with state governments in developing compensated emancipation plans but also called for the colonization of emancipated slaves outside the United States. He also urged Congress to contemplate the inclusion of "free colored people" already in the country in any colonization plan. On March 6, 1862, Lincoln submitted a proposed resolution to Congress recommending the adoption of his plan for compensated emancipation. "Less than one half-day's cost of this war would pay for all the slaves in Delaware at four hundred dollars per head," the president explained to a U.S. senator. Writing to Horace Greeley, the influential newspaper editor, Lincoln confessed, "I am a little uneasy about the abolishment of slavery in this District [of Columbia]…If some one or more of the border-states would move fast, I should greatly prefer it." Although Congress adopted his proposed joint resolution, Lincoln was dismayed at making no further progress among the border state congressmen. The bill emancipating slaves in Washington, D.C., was the best he could expect from these efforts.[15]

Meeting with twenty-nine border state representatives and senators in July, Lincoln appealed to them for broader support for future compensated emancipation legislation before the Congressional recess. "Let the states which are in rebellion see, definitely and certainly, that, in no event, will the states you represent ever join their proposed Confederacy, and they can not, much longer maintain the contest," he reasoned. Two days after this meeting, the border state congressmen jointly declined their support for Lincoln's compensated emancipation plans. Lincoln soon realized that slavery in the border states was not a mere economic concern but rather was strongly entrenched in the societies that used the "peculiar institution" as a means for subjugating those of African descent and where racial prejudice remained deeply ingrained. This would also be true in the rebellious Southern states.[16]

In an effort to make compensated emancipation more palatable to those opposed to it, Lincoln appealed directly to the objects of the issue at hand: persons of color. On August 14, the president met with a local delegation of free African American leaders, urging them to accept his colonization plan as the only solution for themselves and their enslave brethren. It was slavery and their people who were at the basis of the present war, and "[i]t is better for us both… to be separated," the president explained. Although offering the pros and cons for their settlement in Liberia, Lincoln proposed establishing a settlement for them some place in Central America nearer to the United States and similar to the climate of their native land suitable for their physical well-being. Most of the delegation, after a few days of consultation, rejected Lincoln's plans. Frederick Douglass, former slave and famed abolitionist editor, responded in his *Douglass' Monthly* after reading Lincoln's remarks of this meeting:

Illogical and unfair as Mr. Lincoln's statements are, they are nevertheless quite in keeping with his whole course from the beginning of his administration up to this day, and confirm the painful conviction that though elected as an anti-slavery man by Republican and Abolition voters, Mr. Lincoln is quite a genuine representative of American prejudice and Negro hatred and far more concerned for the preservation of slavery, and the favor of the Border Slave States, than for any sentiment of magnanimity or principle of justice and humanity. This address of his leaves us less ground to hope for anti-slavery action at his hands than any of his previous utterances. Notwithstanding his repeated declarations that he considers slavery an evil, every step of his Presidential career relating to slavery proves him active, decided, and brave for its support, and passive, cowardly, and treacherous to the very cause of liberty to which he owes his election. This speech of the President delivered to a committee of free colored men in the capital explains the animus of his interference with the memorable proclamation of General Fremont…He says to the colored people: I don't like you, you must clear out of the country. So too in dealing with anti-slavery Generals the President is direct and firm. He is always brave and resolute in his interferences in favor of slavery, remarkably unconcerned about the wishes and opinions of the people of the north…he is as timid as sheep when required to live up to a single one of his anti-slavery testimonies.[17]

Not deterred by criticisms of his public views, Lincoln responded to an emancipation memorial presented by a delegation of Chicago clergymen on September 13:

What good would a proclamation of emancipation from me do, especially as we are now situated? I do not want to issue a document that the whole world will see must necessarily be inoperative, like the Pope's bull against the comet! Would my word free the slaves, when I cannot even enforce the Constitution in the rebel States?...And what reason is there to think it would have any greater effect upon the slaves than the late law of Congress, which I approved, and which offers protection and freedom to the slaves of rebel masters who come within our lines?...And then unquestionably it would weaken the rebels by drawing off their laborers, which is of great importance. But I am not so sure we could do much with the blacks. If we were to arm them, I fear that in a few weeks the arms would be in the hands of the rebels...There are fifty thousand bayonets in the Union armies from the Border Slave States. It would be a serious matter if, in consequence of a proclamation such as you desire, they should go over to the rebels. I do not think they all would—not so many indeed as a year ago, or as six months ago—not so many to-day as yesterday. Every day increases their Union feeling. They are also getting their pride enlisted, and want to beat the rebels...I think you should admit that we already have an important principle to rally and unite the people in the fact that constitutional government is at stake. This is a fundamental idea, going down about as deep as anything.[18]

If emancipation was to be a part of Lincoln's war effort, what better way to prepare the general public for it than to publicize its flaws and revive the idea of black colonization, which dated back to the late eighteenth century, this time placing the choice and responsibility on persons of color instead of white citizens? Lincoln's oft-quoted response to Horace Greely's *New York Tribune* editorial "The Prayer of Twenty Millions"—taking him to task for not implementing full-scale emancipation—was another step in the process:

My paramount object in this struggle is to save the Union, unless and is not either to save or destroy slavery. If I could save the Union without freeing any slave I would do it, and if I could save it by freeing all the slaves I would do it; and if I could save it by freeing some and leaving others alone I would also do that. What I do about slavery, and the colored race, I do because I believe it helps to save the Union; and what I forbear, I forbear because I do not believe it would help to save the Union. I shall do less whenever I shall believe what I am doing hurts the cause, and I shall do more whenever I shall believe doing more will help the cause. I shall try to

*correct errors when shown to be errors; and I shall adopt new views so fast
as they shall appear to be true views.*

*I have here stated my purpose according to my view of official duty; and
I intend no modification of my oft-expressed personal wish that all men
every where could be free.*[19]

In spite of rhetoric that seemed to either promote conditional emancipation
or seemingly oppose emancipation altogether, Lincoln's thoughts for an
emancipation edict issued by his own authority had been on his mind at the
start of 1862. "I am a patient man," Lincoln wrote to former U.S. senator
Reverdy Johnson, his emissary to Federal-occupied New Orleans, "always
willing to forgive on the Christian terms of repentance; and also to give
ample *time* for repentance. Still I must save this government if possible. What
I cannot do, of course I will not do; but it may as well be understood, once for
all, that I shall not surrender this game leaving any available card unplayed."
It was not a matter of whether emancipation would have some part in his
administration's policies, but rather how much weight emancipation would
have in his primary goal of saving the Union.[20]

Lincoln knew that any executive order he issued on emancipation had to
have the backing of military force. The military campaigns in the eastern
(Virginia) theatre had to score successes to sustain the president's political
priorities. Lincoln had relieved Major General George B. McClellan of his
duties as general in chief in early March 1862 so that the "Young Napoleon"
could concentrate solely on commanding the Army of the Potomac in his
ambitious spring offensive against Confederate forces south of Washington,
D.C. A skilled organizer and able military administrator, McClellan had
already developed the habit of caution and overexaggeration of enemy
strength when confronted by enemy forces. This caused frustration for
Lincoln and many in his cabinet.

McClellan launched his Peninsula Campaign in mid-March 1862,
embarking from Fort Monroe and advancing the Army of the Potomac up
the peninsula between the York and James Rivers toward Richmond. After
a series of battles with Confederates under the overall command of General
Joseph E. Johnston, McClellan sat on the outskirts of the Confederate
capital by late May. On May 31, in what became the Battle of Seven Pines,
Johnston attacked the Federals, halting their progress. In the midst of battle,
Johnston was severely wounded, and Confederate president Jefferson Davis
appointed his military adviser, General Robert E. Lee, to take command of
the Army of Northern Virginia the following day.

Meanwhile, the U.S. War Department had to deal with Confederate forces in Virginia's Shenandoah Valley under Major General Thomas "Stonewall" Jackson that had stymied three separate Federal armies for much of May. Federal troops stationed at Manassas and Fredericksburg were positioned to reinforce McClellan or their comrades in the Shenandoah Valley. All the while, Jackson relieved the pressure of McClellan's forces arrayed against Johnston and, soon after, Lee in Richmond. The arrival of Jackson's troops from the Valley the following month augmented the Army of Northern Virginia's strength. Lincoln, hoping to maintain the offensive, appointed Major General John Pope, who had seen some minor success in the western theatre and was a supporter of Republican Party principles, to organize Federal forces that had been in the Shenandoah Valley, as well as those stationed at Manassas and Fredericksburg, into the short-lived Army of Virginia. This would give the Union war effort two mobile armies against Lee. It was hoped the Army of the Potomac would continue its approach to Richmond from the southeast while the Army of Virginia protected Washington, minimize Confederate activity in the Valley and, if possible, attack Richmond from the northwest in cooperation with McClellan.

Lee, not willing to act in accordance with Lincoln's hopes, launched brutal assaults against the Army of the Potomac, forcing McClellan to withdraw from the environs of Richmond and back to his supply base at Harrison's Landing on the James River. Lincoln arrived at Harrison's Landing on July 7 to confer with McClellan and determine what future role the "Young Napoleon" would play in the campaign against Lee's Confederates. The following day, McClellan handed the president his "Harrison's Landing Letter" outlining his views on political policy of the war. "Military power should not be allowed to interfere with the relations of servitude," McClellan boldly asserted. "A declaration of radical views, especially upon slavery, will rapidly disintegrate our present Armies."[21] Lincoln read the letter, thanked McClellan for it and offered no further verbal responses on the matter. He let his future actions speak for him.

By the time Lincoln returned to Washington, it became clear that any further offensives would fall to Pope and not McClellan. Military policy had to remain subordinate to the president's policies. Lincoln reminded Frémont in Missouri on this and soon reiterated his position to Hunter in South Carolina. In addition to Pope's appointment to command the Army of Virginia, Lincoln appointed Major General Henry W. Halleck, a ranking commander in the western theatre, to the vacant post of general in chief within a day after meeting with McClellan. Lincoln and Secretary of War

Edwin M. Stanton believed that they needed the military expertise of Halleck to coordinate the Federal armies in the field.

Three days after his Harrison's Landing visit, Lincoln shared with Secretary of State William H. Seward and Secretary of the Navy Gideon Welles his early desire to issue an emancipation proclamation while riding in a carriage on its way to the funeral of Secretary Stanton's infant son. "[Lincoln] had given it much thought and had about come to the conclusion that it was a military necessity absolutely essential for the salvation of the Union," Welles recorded in his diary. "[T]hat we must free the slaves or be ourselves or be subdued." In Lincoln's view, it was increasingly clear that the rebellion against the United States would not

Major General Henry W. Halleck (1815–1872) served as general in chief of the United States Army from July 23, 1862, to March 12, 1864, but preferred management from a desk in Washington instead of providing experienced and practical guidance to army commanders in the field such as Burnside. *Library of Congress.*

cease. When asked for their frank opinions, both cabinet officials agreed that emancipation was justified but wanted time to reflect on the subject before rendering decisive answers. Although the navy secretary believed that this was the first time the president mentioned to anyone his plans to emancipate slaves in the rebellious states, Lincoln may have discussed issuing an emancipation proclamation months before with Secretary Stanton and Vice President Hannibal Hamlin on separate occasions. It was also believed that he may have begun drafts of an emancipation document in the War Department's telegraph and cipher room while awaiting news on McClellan's advance toward Richmond.[22]

Lincoln presented a draft of a preliminary emancipation proclamation in a cabinet meeting on July 22. Referencing Congressional acts regarding confiscation of property of rebellious citizens, the document emphasized his desire to provide federal aid to those states implementing voluntary emancipation laws and found in good standing with the United States by the first day of the new year. Otherwise, slaves in these areas would be freed via his war powers authority as commander in chief of the military forces. Acknowledging his cabinet's differing views on emancipation, the president made it clear that his decision to issue an emancipation proclamation was the final word. Nevertheless, he would solicit their suggestions to refine the document. Among the comments and suggestions offered, Secretary Seward recommended Lincoln postpone issuing the emancipation document until Federal forces gained a victory. Given the precarious state of the military situation in Virginia, emancipating slaves that summer might be seen as a desperate act of a fledgling Union war effort and, from Seward's standpoint, could effectively damage relations with European nations poised to recognize the so-called Confederate States of America.[23]

Emancipation hinged on a military victory that Lincoln hoped Pope would secure by late summer. Concerned that Pope's Army of Virginia would unite with McClellan's Army of the Potomac and overwhelm him by sheer numbers, Lee decided to head off Pope's initial advance toward Gordonsville, Virginia, situated along an important Confederate supply route on the Orange and Alexandria Railroad. Although McClellan reluctantly funneled some reinforcements from his own army to Pope, they did not stave off his defeat at Second Bull Run on August 29 and 30.

Lee now had set the stage for what would be his first invasion into the North. He hoped to "liberate" Maryland, a border state, into the Confederacy, as well as encourage foreign recognition and possible intervention, mainly from

Fugitive slaves crossing the Rappahannock River near Warrenton in August 1862. Lincoln issued his Preliminary Emancipation Proclamation on September 22, 1862, five days after the Battle of Antietam (Sharpsburg), convinced that it would break the backbone of the Confederate cause. *Library of Congress.*

Great Britain and France. Pope's retreating forces into Washington, as well as McClellan's evacuated forces from the Virginia Peninsula, prompted Lincoln to appoint McClellan to organize the defense of the capital. Hoping to stem demoralization in the Federal ranks, Lincoln restored the "Young Napoleon" to command of the Army of the Potomac and charged him with the pursuit of Lee. The resulting Maryland Campaign that culminated and ended with the Battle of Antietam (Sharpsburg) on September 17 became the bloodiest day so far in the war, with twenty-three thousand casualties total from both sides. Although the Federals held the battlefield in a tactical victory, Lee withdrew his forces back across the Potomac River. Acting on Seward's suggestion in July, Lincoln issued the Preliminary Emancipation Proclamation five days after Antietam.

Frederick Douglass (1818–1895), an escaped Maryland slave, was a prominent abolitionist and editor who was one of Lincoln's harshest critics on his slow progress in making emancipation a part of the Union war effort. Once the Preliminary Emancipation Proclamation was issued, Douglass would become one of his most enthusiastic supporters. *Library of Congress.*

The Preliminary Emancipation Proclamation issued on September 22, 1862, was very similar to the document Lincoln had read to his cabinet earlier that summer. The difference was that primary authority for issuing it came from his position as commander in chief. Lincoln asserted that "the war will be prosecuted for the object of practically restoring the constitutional relation between the United States, and each of the states, and the people there of, in which states that relation is, or may be suspended, or disturbed." Slaves in states or portions of states still in rebellion by January 1, 1863, would be freed, and the maintenance of their status would be guaranteed by the U.S. military. Lincoln would also recommend to Congress appropriate funding to those slave states that end the rebellion and voluntarily adopt "immediate, or gradual abolishment of slavery within their respective limits." Individuals in these areas in rebellion who had remained loyal to the Union would receive compensation for their loss in property, including slaves. Moreover, he would continue colonization efforts that would remove persons of African descent outside the country.[24]

When news of the emancipation spread to the states of the Confederacy, Robert E. Lee, attempting to rebuild his command after Antietam, shared his views with Confederate president Jefferson Davis in early October. "The military government of the United States has been so perfected by the recent proclamations of President Lincoln, which you have no doubt seen, and civil liberty so completely trodden under foot," he wrote, "that I have strong hopes that the conservative portion of that people, unless dead to the feelings of liberty, will rise and depose the party now in power." Coupled with the hope of a counterrevolution in the Union, Confederate citizens hoped that the Lincoln's measures would increase the ranks of the Confederate armies. "This will only intensify the war, and add largely to our numbers in the field," concluded John B. Jones, a civilian employee in the Confederate War Department in Richmond. It was his belief that Lincoln's future Emancipation Proclamation would "seal the doom of one hundred thousand of his own people!" The ranks of Lee's Army of Northern Virginia did, in fact, increase that fall.[25]

While the Confederacy viewed Lincoln's proclamation with obvious disdain, the Northern population proved even more troubling on the subject of emancipation. Reception of emancipation remained positive for most Republicans, particularly those of moderate or conservative bent, when compensated emancipation and colonization were thrown into the political mix. The faction of Northern Democrats soon to be labeled "Peace Democrats," favoring a toleration of slavery and peaceful compromise with the Southern states, made significant gains in the fall midterm Congressional and state contests. Republicans maintained slight majorities in the House of Representatives and the Senate, but Democrats increased their House seats from forty-four to seventy-two. Democrats also made significant gains in statewide elections in Pennsylvania, New York, Ohio, Illinois and Indiana. U.S. troops dispatched to these Northern states had to suppress overt resistance to emancipation as a war aim and enforce recruitment quotas for state militias. It was these very states that supplied the greater number of volunteers to the Federal armies.[26]

McClellan proved to be as much of a political thorn in Lincoln's side as he continued to be a military thorn. Feeling as much despair over the recent

Lincoln and Major General George B. McClellan (1826–1885) conferred on October 3, 1862, near the Antietam Battlefield. Lincoln accused McClellan of having a case of the "slows" in failing to pursue and destroy the Confederate army under Robert E. Lee. *Library of Congress.*

proclamation as the Northern public, McClellan contemplated whether or not to publish Lincoln's order to the Army of the Potomac and went as far as to draft a letter to the president expressing his views that emancipation was a poor policy that the army should not enforce. Wiser political allies persuaded "Little Mac" from sending this correspondence, as they believed it bordered on treason. Nevertheless, McClellan's views were shared by many of his subordinate generals, who counseled their chief to let the army continue performing its duty in spite of an unpopular policy. Although McClellan expressed political and military views contrary to Lincoln's, there was little to no evidence that the commander of the Army of the Potomac ever made serious contemplation of staging a military coup against the administration. On the other hand, McClellan's lack of movement in pursuing Lee after Antietam only increased the perception that a conspiracy against Lincoln in the wake of the fall elections was afoot. In one instance, McClellan argued that his army lacked adequate supplies and that his horses were fatigued and in very poor condition to resume active operations against Lee. Lincoln replied to his cautious general, "Will you pardon me for asking what the horses of your army have done since the battle of Antietam that fatigue anything?" After repeated failed attempts to prod McClellan into action, Lincoln, who accused him for having a case of the "slows," had had enough.

On the snowy evening of November 7, Brigadier General Cathernius P. Buckingham, a senior staff officer of the War Department, arrived at the headquarters of Major General Ambrose E. Burnside, commanding the IX Corps near Orlean in central Virginia, with important dispatches from the War Department that relieved McClellan of command in favor of Burnside. Burnside had twice turned down command of the Army of the Potomac. Initially protesting the order, Burnside acquiesced on the apparent belief that if he declined command that it would go to Major General Joseph Hooker commanding the V Corps, whom he did not like.[27]

Secretary of the Navy Gideon Welles believed that Burnside would "doubtless do his best, is patriotic and amiable, and had he greater powers and grasp, would make an acceptable and popular, if not, a great, general." Captain Charles Francis Adams Jr. of the First Massachusetts Cavalry, the grandson and great-grandson of U.S. presidents, wrote to his younger brother, "The army believed in McClellan, but the Generals are jealous and ambitious and little, and want to get a step themselves, so they are willing to see him pulled down." McClellan had not been exceptionally brilliant (but prudent), and it took time for any general to be able to manage a large army. Adams's greatest fear was that "now a new man must learn...by his own mistakes and in the blood of the army."[28]

Many soldiers in the Army of the Potomac recalled McClellan's departure from the army in the most emotional terms. Some disgruntled soldiers expressed the hope within the confines of their campfires and among regimental comrades that McClellan would disobey his orders and march the army to Washington, setting up a dictatorship. "I have heard a good deal about how the soldiers idolized Little Mac and resented his dismissal from command," recalled a Massachusetts soldier, "but I heard nothing of the sort in my regiment...they were quite ready to try some one else." Lincoln had suspicions that subversive elements, not necessarily McClellan, were influencing the Army of the Potomac. McClellan's continued presence and strong identification with that army would cause further problems for his authority as commander in chief in the wake of the recent midterm elections and lukewarm to negative reception of his emancipation policy for many in the North. Major General George G. Meade, a division commander with the army, wrote to his wife, explaining that had McClellan been dismissed immediately after Antietam, "I could have seen some show of reason on *military* grounds." But the dismissal coming after the New York elections "proves conclusively that the cause is political," Meade continued.[29]

In addition to replacing McClellan with Burnside in the eastern theatre, the recent Congressional elections also allowed Lincoln to make a significant command change in the western theatre. A week before McClellan's removal, Lincoln relieved Major General Don Carlos Buell of his command of the Army of the Ohio. A staunch McClellan supporter, Buell had earned Lincoln's ire by failing to pursue the Confederate army under General Braxton Bragg into Tennessee after the Battle of Perryville, Kentucky. He was replaced by the eccentric Major General William S. Rosecrans, and the Army of the Ohio eventually became the Army of the Cumberland. In making these command changes, Lincoln hoped to sustain emancipation as a war aim through substantial military victories in both theatres by the end of the year. Much attention would be given to Burnside's Army of the Potomac and its future operations against Lee in Virginia.[30]

In his Annual Message to Congress on December 1, 1862, Lincoln still held out the hope that the border states would embrace emancipation by proposing three constitutional amendments. One proposed amendment would compensate states for the loss of slaves if such states passed emancipation laws before January 1, 1863. The second proposed amendment dealt with individual compensation to slaveholders who had maintained their loyalty to the Union. The third proposed amendment reiterated his desire for Congressional appropriations to colonize free persons of color by their own consent to any place outside the United States. "Without slavery the rebellion could never have existed," Lincoln added. "Without slavery it could not continue."

In spite of the recent elections and political backlash from the Preliminary Proclamation, emancipation was now a key war aim, and Lincoln would not turn back. "In *giving* freedom to the *slave*," he reasoned, "we *assure* freedom to the *free*." Thinking toward the military operations he hoped to move forward to enforce emancipation before winter came, Lincoln proclaimed, "We know how to save the Union. The world knows we do know how to save it." Ambrose Burnside, commanding the premier Federal Army of the Potomac, would be the key instrument in saving the Union through enforcing emancipation. "Fellow citizens," Lincoln proclaimed, "*we* cannot escape history."[31]

Frederick Douglass, an early Lincoln critic, endorsed the Preliminary Proclamation in an October editorial:

> *Abraham Lincoln may be slow, Abraham Lincoln may desire peace even at the price of leaving our terrible national sore untouched…but Abraham Lincoln is not the man to reconsider, retract and contradict words and purposes solemnly proclaimed over his official signature.*
>
> *The careful, and we think, the slothful deliberation which he has observed in reaching this obvious policy, is a guarantee against retraction. But even if the temper and spirit of the President himself were other than what they are, events greater than the President, events which have slowly wrung this proclamation from him may be relied on to carry him forward in the same direction.*[32]

For Douglass, events clearly controlled the activities of Abraham Lincoln for the better.

Chapter 2

The Great Object of the Campaign

Armies in a Virginia Winter

The most identifiable military unit in both the Federal and Confederate armies in the Civil War was the regiment. A regiment of infantry consisted of ten companies of one hundred soldiers each. Although the standard complement of an infantry regiment was theoretically one thousand, it often stood at half this number for both sides due to soldier deaths and absences from sickness and detached duty. Regiments usually represented a particular region or, at times, an individual county of a state, with companies made up of citizens from different localities of that region or county. Commissioned officers with the rank of captain commanded companies assisted by first and second lieutenants, while colonels commanded regiments assisted by lieutenant colonels and majors. Military formations at the regimental level were universal throughout both Federal and Confederate armies.

Federal infantry brigades, made up of two to seven regiments, constituted the largest military formation of a single combat arm. Commanded by brigadier generals, brigades averaged 1,500 to 3,000 men by 1862. Usually three brigades formed an infantry division under a major general. One to four artillery batteries were attached to an infantry division. Three divisions generally made up a corps under a major general, and a corps was the largest maneuverable unit for combat operations. Unlike their Confederate counterparts, the Federal army tended to be somewhat stingy in bestowing general officer rank beyond major general. Confederate divisions tended to be larger, having one or two additional brigades than

Federal divisions commanded by major generals, while Confederate corps commanded by lieutenant generals contained one or more additional divisions than Federal corps.[33]

Ambrose E. Burnside and the Army of the Potomac had been given the difficult task of launching an offensive campaign against Robert E. Lee and the Army of Northern Virginia before winter weather ceased all military operations. Historically, armies in war very rarely fought in the winter due to poor weather conditions affecting the health of soldiers, difficult road conditions slowing the transportation of troops and supplies over frozen and mud-clogged roads and the lack of abundant natural resources needed for food, fuel and shelter that would have to wait until spring. "I wish they [the Federals] would fight or let it alone, one or the other, so we could get into winter quarters," wrote William R. Stilwell of the 53rd Georgia Infantry, "for just as long as they keep moving about we will have to do the same." As both armies eventually faced each other on opposite sides of the Rappahannock River at Fredericksburg, Francis Adams Donaldson of the 118th Pennsylvania Infantry speculated, "It looks very much as though we would winter quarter here."[34]

Robert E. Lee held strong connections to Fredericksburg and the surrounding area prior to 1862. William Fitzhugh, who had built the prominent Chatham Manor across the river, was the maternal grandfather of Lee's wife, Mary Anna Randolph Custis, and it had been speculated, but not substantiated, that young Robert had courted Mary on a visit to the two-storied red bricked mansion. Lee's father-in-law, George Washington Parke Custis, was the grandson of Martha Dandridge Custis Washington and adopted grandson of her husband, George Washington. Marrying Mary Custis in 1831, Lee increased not only his stature within Virginia society but also his connections to the much revered George Washington. Washington had grown up across the Rappahannock at nearby Ferry Farm. As an adult, Washington established a home in Fredericksburg for his widowed mother, Mary Ball Washington.[35]

Lee's father, Henry "Light Horse Harry" Lee, had earned Washington's praise for his combat effectiveness as the Continental army's most resourceful light dragoon commander in the American Revolution. Unfortunately, by the time young Robert was born in 1807, Henry Lee's reputation was in shambles. Both father and son admired George Washington. The younger Lee used Washington as his role model because, and in spite, of his father's tumultuous history. Even in the midst of the Civil War, comparisons between Washington and Lee were being made and often illuminated by the commander of the Army of Northern Virginia himself.[36]

The Great Object of the Campaign

Lee graduated second in the West Point class of 1829 without accumulating a single demerit for infractions. Posted to the army's prestigious corps of engineers, Lieutenant (and, later, Captain) Lee pursued his military tasks in planning and constructing military forts along the eastern seaboard and navigation projects along the Mississippi River.[37] The short-lived Black Hawk War in 1832 and the continuing Seminole Wars in Florida bypassed Lee as his brother officers gained actual combat experience. At age forty, Lee experienced his first taste of combat in the Mexican-American War, earning three brevet battlefield promotions and prompting General Winfield Scott to write in an official report:

> *I am impelled to make special mention of the services of Captain R.E. Lee, engineers. This officer, greatly distinguished in the siege of Vera Cruz, was again indefatigable, during these operations, in reconnaissances as daring as laborious, and of the greatest value. Nor was he less conspicuous in planting batteries, and in conducting columns to their sections under the heavy fire of the enemy.*[38]

Lee continued to serve in the engineers until his 1852 appointment as superintendent of his alma mater, West Point. Among the cadets who attended the academy during Lee's superintendence were his oldest son Custis Lee; J.E.B. Stuart, future Army of Northern Virginia cavalry commander; his nephew Fitzhugh Lee, later serving as a cavalry brigade commander under Stuart; and Oliver O. Howard, a future division commander in the Federal Army of the Potomac, leading one of the assaults against Marye's Heights at Fredericksburg.[39] In March 1855, Lee was appointed lieutenant colonel of the newly created Second U.S. Cavalry regiment and spent the bulk of two years on the Texas frontier, conducting expeditions primarily against the Comanche tribe. The death of his father-in-law, George Washington Parke Custis, enabled Colonel Lee to be granted a leave of absence from the army in 1857 to return to Arlington House in Virginia to settle Custis's affairs as one of his executors.[40]

In mid-October 1859, Lee found himself thrust into the national spotlight when Lieutenant J.E.B. Stuart of the First U.S. Cavalry, on leave from his regiment, arrived at Arlington with a summons for Lee to go to the War Department. After conferring with his superiors, Lee and Stuart rode to Harpers Ferry, Virginia, on October 17. Lee took command of a detachment of U.S. Marines and various militia units from Virginia and Maryland in order to put down an apparent slave revolt and recapture the U.S. Arsenal at Harpers Ferry. Many of the twenty-two black and white insurgents seeking to free Virginia's slaves had been killed in the initial raid, and a small number, along with their leader, John Brown, were barricaded in the arsenal's engine house. Lee ordered an assault of the building by the marines, freeing hostages captured in the ill-fated raid and taking Brown and his remaining followers into custody.[41]

Returning to the Harpers Ferry area in December to take charge of federal troops to quell any abolitionist attempts, real or imagined, to rescue John Brown, Lee had previously reflected on the volatile issue of slavery and its expansion into the territories acquired from Mexico in the late war. Writing to his wife, Lee stated:

> *In this enlightened age, there are few I believe, but will acknowledge, that slavery as an institution is a moral & political evil in any Country[.] It is useless to expatiate on its disadvantages. I think it however a greater evil to the white than to the black race, & while my feelings are strongly enlisted in behalf of the latter, my sympathies are more strong for the former...While we see the Course of the final abolition of human Slavery is onward, & we give it all the aid of our prayers & all justifiable means in our power, we must leave the progress as well as the result in his hands who sees the end; who Choose to work by slow influences; & with whom two thousand years are but a single day.*[42]

Resuming active duty in early 1860, Lee commanded cavalry at Fort Mason, Texas, as sectional tensions culminated with South Carolina passing its ordinance of secession from the United States on December 20, 1860, in the wake of Abraham Lincoln's election as the nation's sixteenth president. Lee, ordered to Washington in light of the recent secession of Southern states, received promotion to colonel, commanding the First U.S. Cavalry.[43]

General in Chief Winfield Scott, a fellow Virginian who considered Lee one of the most gifted officers in the army, encouraged Lee to accept command of the army used to put down the imminent rebellion. Lee maintained his position that he would not draw his sword against his native Virginia if it left the Union. On April 22, 1861, Virginia left the Union, and Lee resigned his commission after thirty-two years in the U.S. Army. Writing to his longtime mentor Winfield Scott, Lee stated gracefully, "I shall carry to the grave the most grateful recollections of your kind consideration, and your name and fame will always be dear to me."[44]

Shortly after his resignation from the U.S. Army, Lee accepted a major general's commission and command of Virginia's military and naval forces.

The Great Object of the Campaign

The new Confederate president, Jefferson Davis of Mississippi, appointed Lee, among several others, as full generals in the Provisional Army of the Confederate States. Lee began his initial service organizing the coastal defenses in South Carolina and Georgia, as well as coordinating Confederate military operations in western Virginia. He ultimately served as Davis's chief military advisor until the fateful day of June 1, 1862, when his West Point classmate, General Joseph E. Johnson, was severely wounded in action, and President Davis ordered Lee to take command of the Army of Northern Virginia. Lee quickly earned his high reputation through victories over McClellan on the Peninsula and over Pope at Second Manassas. Fighting McClellan at Antietam forced Lee to take his army back into Virginia. When he heard of McClellan's replacement by Ambrose Burnside, Lee remarked, "We [he and McClellan] always understood each other so well...I fear they may continue to make these changes till they find some one whom I don't understand."[45]

Lieutenant Colonel E. Porter Alexander, who would command a Confederate artillery battalion on Marye's Heights at Fredericksburg, recalled a conversation he had had with a staff officer early in the war about Lee. He told Alexander that Lee bested all commanders,

General Robert E. Lee (1807–1870) commanded the Army of Northern Virginia and held nominal responsibility for Confederate operations throughout Virginia. In five short months, Lee had forged a successful field army that earned a high reputation throughout the Confederacy and frustrated Federal forces arrayed against it. *Minnis & Cowell, Virginia Historical Society, Richmond, Virginia.*

Major General Ambrose E. Burnside (1824–1881) turned down command of the Army of the Potomac on two occasions but reluctantly agreed to take command on November 7, 1862, because of his apparent dislike of Joseph Hooker, who would have been next in line for command. *Library of Congress.*

Federal and Confederate, in audacity. "Lee is audacity personified," the staff officer proclaimed. "His name is audacity, and you need not be afraid of not seeing all of it that you will want to see." Unfortunately, Alexander could not apply audacity to Ambrose Burnside, the Army of the Potomac's new commander who succeeded McClellan. "Burnside was a man almost universally popular, though few thought, & he did not apparently think himself, any great general," Alexander explained, remembering Burnside's reputation. "In my mind his name is associated with 'Benny Havens's' near West Point, for he was old Benny's greatest admiration of all cadets ever at the Academy." The tavern run by Benny Havens for several decades remained a landmark institution of the military academy. Located at nearby Buttermilk (Highland) Falls, New York, Havens had served beer, spirits and food to generations of cadets before the Civil War, to the chagrin of West Point officials. Burnside's reputation at West Point had continued to be a much discussed topic after his graduation ten years later, when Alexander graduated.[46]

Born in Liberty, Indiana, in 1824, Ambrose Everts Burnside was named for a deceased child of the doctor who delivered him. He was the son of a local judge and state legislator who, with his wife, had originally hailed from South Carolina but had moved to the Midwest due to their distaste for slavery. Apprenticed as a tailor, young Ambrose "was of an ardent and adventurous character, with an active and sanguine temperament, which hardly suited to a quiet occupation" one biographer noted. Through his father's influence, young Burnside received an appointment to West Point in the summer of 1843.[47]

Among Burnside's classmates who would serve under him at Fredericksburg were Orlando B. Willcox, commanding the IX Corps; John Gibbon, a division commander in the I Corps; Charles Griffin, a division commander in the V Corps; Thomas H. Neill, a brigade commander in the VI Corps; and William W. Burns, a division commander in the IX Corps. Classmate Ambrose Powell Hill of Virginia commanded one of the largest divisions in Lee's Army of Northern Virginia. Both Gibbon and Hill had been members of the class of 1846 but were held back to the following year due to illness. Another classmate, Henry Heth from Virginia, would not join Lee's Confederate army until 1863 but was Burnside's best friend and roommate while at the academy.[48]

Although the fun-loving and gregarious Cadet Burnside made friends easily while at West Point, his conduct proved contrary to the rigorous and strict discipline that governed the academy, although it seemed his instructors liked him as much as the other cadets. Taking up the forbidden vices of smoking and drinking, Burnside had a penchant for unauthorized absences from the post, failure to perform routine duties, talking while on guard duty, unauthorized visiting and committing pranks against his fellow cadets.

Graduating in 1847, Brevet Second Lieutenant Burnside was assigned initially to the Second U.S. Artillery and, following his summer furlough, traveled in company with some of his graduated classmates to New Orleans for eventual duty in Mexico, where war had been raging for a year. By the time Burnside arrived in Mexico, he had been assigned as a permanent second lieutenant in the Third U.S. Artillery. Burnside—leading a detachment of recruits for the Third Artillery who were responsible for escorting and protecting a mule-drawn baggage train from bands of marauding Mexican troops—traced the path taken by General Winfield Scott on his recently celebrated campaign from Veracruz to Mexico City, taking in some of the battle sites he had missed by only a few months.[49]

By the time Burnside arrived in Mexico City, the Mexican-American War was virtually over, and Burnside, like many of his fellow officers, served in a demobilizing army that was tedious in routine and left room open for the pursuit of the very vices that West Point had frowned on. While some officers took to excessive drinking, others spent time in gambling establishments. Burnside gained notoriety for the latter vice, increasing the stakes when holding a losing hand. When the Treaty of Guadeloupe-Hidalgo was finalized in February 1848, officially ending the war, Burnside owed six months' pay in gambling debts.[50]

That same year, Burnside was transferred back to the United States and stationed at Fort Adams near Newport, Rhode Island, where he enjoyed almost a year of civilization and active society that kept him from delving into the realm of indulging in the improper vices to which he had been accustomed in Mexico. In 1849, Burnside was sent with his unit to the remote post of Las Vegas, New Mexico Territory, located along the Santa Fe Trail and forty miles east of Santa Fe. Although a light artillery unit, Burnside and his men were equipped as a cavalry detachment providing general escort duty, protecting U.S. mail trains and performing scouting missions.[51]

Burnside, as commissioned officers were scarce commodities, often found himself having the extra duty of serving as his post's quartermaster and commissary officer. Since he was away for lengthy periods of time on escort duty, Burnside would authorize and sign advanced requisitions of considerable sums that he forwarded to higher headquarters at Santa Fe. He placed great faith in the departmental quartermaster, who would expend only the necessary supplies needed to keep the fort running in his absence. Unfortunately, the departmental quartermaster either erroneously or unscrupulously handled the unexpended governmental funds, which caused federal auditors to present Burnside with a bill for payment of well over $6,000 a few years later.[52]

Among the threats to mail wagons along the Santa Fe Trail were bands of Apaches, who proved resilient adversaries to U.S. Army detachments. Leading his detachment of twenty-nine soldiers in a charge attack against sixty members of a marauding band of Jicarilla Apaches in August 1849, Burnside routed the group, killing eighteen and ending up with an arrow in his neck just below the ear for his efforts. He received praise from his post commander, as well as from the departmental commander for the New Mexico Territory. Realizing from this experience that the only effective weapon his mounted troops had to combat the fast moving Apaches were their sabers in close quarters combat, Burnside began developing an idea for a light cavalry carbine loaded from the breech. Revolvers were not standard issue during this time, and muzzleloading weapons were too awkward to handle on horseback in the midst of a running battle.[53]

After a leave of absence, Burnside returned to duty in April 1851, serving on the commission charged with marking out the boundary between the United States and Mexico as stipulated in the Treaty of Guadeloupe-Hidalgo that ended the war between the two nations. Ordered back to Fort Adams, Rhode Island, in March 1852, Burnside married Mary Richmond Bishop of Providence. The former Ms. Bishop might have been the key element in Burnside's ability to refrain from his vices during his first tour at Fort Adams four years earlier. No sooner had he married than Burnside's blank vouchers to the departmental quartermaster in New Mexico began to become an annoying issue for the lieutenant, as the government mistakenly sought him out to satisfy the outstanding debts. In the midst of trying to improve his economic situation in providing for his household and seeing his dream of developing an effective carbine firearm, Burnside resigned from the U.S. Army in October 1853.[54]

Moving to nearby Bristol, Burnside channeled his idea of creating an effective cavalry firearm into a business venture by establishing the Bristol Rifle Works. His design that became the "Burnside breech loader" carbine, and its counterpart rifle, would produce one of the best weapons of its type in use. More than fifty-five thousand of his carbines would be in service during the Civil War. Although initial sales were sluggish, Secretary of War Jefferson Davis purchased a small number for the army, and others were purchased for use as sporting rifles. By 1857, Davis's successor, John B. Floyd, made verbal agreements with Burnside for future government contracts amounting to $90,000, provided his weapons met board-certified testing. Burnside, competing with other weapon inventors, returned to his alma mater for the board to test his weapon. Captain Henry Heth of the Tenth U.S. Infantry, Burnside's West Point roommate, served on the board and judged it along with the other members to be the "best suited for military service." Unfortunately, Secretary Floyd's verbal promises went unfulfilled, with contracts going to his personal friends instead of Burnside. Unable to maintain his business and pay his creditors, Burnside put much of his personal items up for collateral, foregoing a declaration of bankruptcy, and sought to repay his outstanding debts.[55]

Writing to George B. McClellan, who had been a year ahead of him at West Point, Burnside inquired of the former army officer turned executive of the Illinois Central Railroad about any positions with the railroads. McClellan gladly offered him a position with his own railroad as a cashier for the land department. Confiding to his wife, McClellan derived great satisfaction in helping his old friend. "Why, that honest, true, brave old Burnside is worth a legion of those paltry butterflies that flutter around ballrooms," he wrote. "If ever a man went to heaven he [Burnside] will surely go there." Soon elevated to vice-president of the railroad, McClellan welcomed Burnside and his wife to share their spacious home on Chicago's lakefront. For the next two years, Burnside steadily paid off his debts and was promoted to treasurer of the railroad's office in New York, where he was able to afford his own accommodations. By 1860, the Burnsides continued commuting between New York City and Providence.[56]

Called on by the Rhode Island governor to command state troops, Burnside accepted his appointment as colonel of the First Rhode Island Infantry at the start of the Civil War. By July 1861, Burnside commanded a four-regiment brigade in McDowell's Federal force heading for Manassas Junction. He and his brigade had a sound performance at First Bull Run that earned him a promotion to brigadier general of volunteers.[57]

In October, Burnside was charged with organizing a "Coast Division" assembling at Annapolis, Maryland, for an expedition to the North Carolina coast. Between January and May 1862, Burnside's forces captured major strategic points along the northeastern coast of North Carolina, bringing them under Federal control. His reputation with the Lincoln administration was on the rise as McClellan's fortunes on the James River dimmed by the late summer due, in part, to the fact that he had made no major mistakes in independent command.[58]

By late August, Burnside was headquartered across the Rappahannock from Fredericksburg acting as a liaison and troop manager, funneling reinforcements from McClellan's army to Pope's. In the meantime, the majority of his Coast Division was transferred to Virginia, augmented by reinforcements and renamed the IX Army Corps. After the Federal debacle of Second Bull Run, McClellan incorporated Burnside and his IX Corps into his reorganized Army of the Potomac as Lee's Confederates ventured into Maryland. It was at Antietam that Burnside received his first major criticism of his abilities as a combat commander. Burnside served as a "wing" commander, although McClellan removed Hooker's I Corps from his authority. In actuality, Burnside commanded a wing that was composed solely of his own IX Corps. Brigadier General Jacob D. Cox, in temporary command of the corps, offered to step down, but Burnside declined, not accepting the slight from his old friend, and simply became an additional headquarters through which orders passed from the army commander down to Cox or simply "an awkward diffusion of command responsibility."[59]

The battle that occurred on September 17 was fought in three distinct phases throughout the day. Burnside spearheaded the Federal efforts of the third phase of battle that afternoon, operating on the right flank of the Confederate line. It was here that the IX Corps faced the obstacle of Antietam Creek, with only a 125-foot-long triple-arched stone bridge (Lower Bridge or Rohrbach Bridge or, soon after, Burnside's Bridge) as the most direct means of crossing. Burnside had already received stern rebukes from McClellan's headquarters for the slow pace in getting his men into action both at South Mountain and at Antietam. Whether McClellan's observations were well founded or not, Burnside chose the path of least resistance and followed his orders to the letter.

Antietam Creek ran narrowly in the vicinity of the Lower Bridge, and the superior number of Federals could have easily crossed the creek. The problem was in the terrain. The Rohrbach Road, once it crossed the bridge, led to higher bluffs looking down on the bridge. A small force of Confederate Georgians held the bluffs roughly on three sides, overlooking the bridge and creek. Regardless of how many Federal troops attempted to cross the bridge or creek, they became clear and open enemy targets. Hoping to fix the attention of the Georgians at the bridge with a portion of the IX Corps, Burnside ordered a division under Brigadier General Isaac Rodman to cross Antietam Creek at a ford two-thirds of a mile below the bridge to flank the enemy. Due to the lack of proper reconnaissance by either Burnside's or McClellan's headquarters, Rodman's men discovered that the ford was virtually impossible to negotiate due to steep bluffs. In its continued search for a suitable crossing, Rodman's division would be out of contact and unavailable in Burnside's attempt to cross the bridge. By the time Rodman's men crossed Antietam Creek farther down than they had intended and Burnside forced a crossing of the Lower Bridge, the timely arrival of A.P. Hill's "Light Division" from Harpers Ferry halted the IX Corps' advance on the Confederate right, saving Lee's army from destruction.

After a month in the northern Shenandoah Valley, Lee's army, still in need of forage, sent Longstreet's command to Culpeper, east of the Blue Ridge Mountains, while Major General Thomas "Stonewall" Jackson's command established camp a few miles northeast of Winchester but remained in the Valley. Major General J.E.B. Stuart's cavalry was ordered to seek forage east of the mountains in Loudoun and Fauquier Counties. From intelligence reports, the Federal Army of the Potomac was slowly advancing south from the vicinity of Harpers Ferry toward Warrenton between the base of the Blue Ridge Mountains and the Orange and Alexandria Railroad. On November 7, Lee reported the capture of Warrenton by Federal forces. Believing that the enemy's strength would decrease as they advanced, Lee hoped "an opportunity will offer for us to strike a successful blow."[60] At best, Lee would be able to muster between seventy-eight and eighty thousand men should the Army of the Potomac launch an offensive before winter firmly set in. This is the maximum number of troops he would eventually have at Fredericksburg in December.[61] After Antietam, Lee recommended to President Davis the elevation of Longstreet and Jackson to corps command, with promotions for both to lieutenant general, which was granted in early

November. This command structure would remain in effect in the Army of Northern Virginia until after the Chancellorsville Campaign in the spring of 1863.[62]

James Longstreet, commanding the First Corps, became Lee's chief subordinate in the army as a result of his promotion being made a day before Jackson's. Hailing from Edgefield District, South Carolina, where he was born in 1821, Longstreet resided in Georgia. Longstreet received an appointment to West Point from an Alabama congressman and entered the military academy in 1838. As a child, young James had been nicknamed "Peter" or "Pete," and this sobriquet transformed itself into "Old Peter" or "Old Pete" while at West Point. Graduating in 1842 two ranks from the bottom of his class, Longstreet was assigned a brevet second lieutenant to the Fourth U.S. Infantry stationed at Jefferson Barracks, Missouri.[63] In 1844, Longstreet, along with his regiment, was transferred to Louisiana. Promoted to permanent second lieutenant the following year, he was assigned to the Eighth U.S. Infantry stationed in Florida. His tour in Florida was brief, as the Eighth was ordered to Corpus Christi, Texas, as part of General Zachary Taylor's Army of Observation in the prelude to the Mexican-American War. Lieutenant Longstreet fought under Taylor in all the battles in northern Mexico throughout 1846 and under General Winfield Scott in his advance from Veracruz to Mexico City the following year. At the storming of Chapultepec Heights, Longstreet (having been promoted to first lieutenant) led the front ranks with the regimental flag in hand before being struck down in the thigh by an enemy musket ball. Handing the flag to Lieutenant George E. Pickett of his regiment, who carried it over the wall of the fortress, Longstreet was out of commission for the rest of the war. He was brevetted a captain and major for his efforts.[64] After a slow recuperation back in the states, Longstreet returned to duty with the Eighth Infantry and married Maria Louise Garland, daughter of Brevet Brigadier General John Garland, his commanding officer, in 1848. Serving at Carlisle Barracks in Pennsylvania and various posts in Texas and New Mexico Territory, Longstreet was promoted to the permanent rank of major and assigned as an army paymaster in 1858.[65]

Joining the Confederacy with a lieutenant colonel's commission, Longstreet received rapid promotion to brigadier general in command of a brigade of Virginia regiments in time for First Manassas (First Bull Run). As one of General Joseph E. Johnson's senior generals in the infant Army of Northern Virginia during the early phases of the Peninsula Campaign, Longstreet proved a dependable presence in battle. Lee recognized this

Lieutenant General James Longstreet (1821–1904), Lee's "Old War Horse" and senior subordinate, commanded the First Corps of the Army of Northern Virginia. His troops were responsible for inflicting the highest number of casualties on the Army of the Potomac at Fredericksburg. *Museum of the Confederacy, Richmond, Virginia.*

Lieutenant General Thomas J. "Stonewall" Jackson (1824–1863) was arguably the most popular Confederate general in 1862 and commanded the Second Corps of the Army of Northern Virginia. He commanded Confederates in the most desperate portion of the Fredericksburg Battlefield. *National Archives.*

trait when he assumed command of the army. Longstreet commanded the "Right Wing" of the army at Second Manassas (Second Bull Run) and at Sharpsburg (Antietam). It was in the aftermath of the latter battle that Lee greeted Longstreet riding toward him with: "Here comes my war horse just from the field he has done so much to save."[66] The title of "Lee's War Horse" remained with the First Corps commander for the rest of his natural days. "Old Peter" would become the foundation of Lee's army for much of its better days.

Thomas Jonathan "Stonewall" Jackson, commanding the Second Corps of Lee's army, had garnered more fame than his superior had so far in the war. Born near Clarksburg, Virginia (now West Virginia), in 1824, Jackson was a member of the West Point class of 1846.[67] Beginning West Point at an educational disadvantage compared to most of his classmates, Jackson gradually rose in his class standing by sheer perseverance and emerged ranking seventeenth out of fifty-nine cadets upon graduation. He had already earned the nicknames "Old Jack" and "General."[68] Assigned to the First U.S. Artillery, Lieutenant Jackson, like many of his classmates, immediately embarked to the seat of war in Mexico. Brevetted three times for his skillful management of artillery under intense fire, "Major" Jackson had fought in all of General Winfield Scott's engagements in his march from Veracruz to Mexico City. Once Mexico City was occupied, Jackson, on a formal occasion, was presented to General Scott, who replied, "I don't know if I will shake hands with Mr. Jackson!" Jackson was momentarily taken aback. "If you can forgive yourself for the way in which you slaughtered those poor Mexicans with your guns," Scott continued with his compliment, "I am not sure that I can."[69]

Jackson returned to the United States after the war, serving in Florida under Captain William H. French, who would command a II Corps division at Fredericksburg. Both men proffered charges against the other over a series of disputes that wore the patience of their army superiors. Eventually, Jackson received an appointment as a professor at the Virginia Military Institute (VMI) in 1851, ending his career in the Old Army and allowing him to establish roots in Lexington, Virginia. A decade later, Major Jackson, casting his lot with the Confederacy, escorted a contingent of VMI cadets to serve as drill instructors to the mass of Virginia volunteers congregating in Richmond.[70]

By the end of April 1861, Jackson had taken command of Confederate forces at Harpers Ferry. Promoted to brigadier general, "Old Jack," as his soldiers called him, reminiscent of his West Point days, spent much of the following month in nearby Winchester at the northern end of Virginia's Shenandoah Valley. As part of General Joseph E. Johnson's command at First Manassas (First Bull Run), the former VMI instructor earned his famous nickname. On that fateful afternoon of July 21, the Federal forces of General Irwin McDowell had hounded Confederate forces from the prominent battlefield landmark Henry Hill. Jackson had ordered his brigade to lie prone on the reverse slope of the hill, at the edge of a nearby wood, for protection against Federal artillery, as Brigadier General Barnard Bee of South Carolina galloped forward, reporting, "General, they [the Federals] are driving us!" Jackson replied, "Sir, we will give them the bayonet." The South Carolinian returned to his entangled Confederate command and, pointing his sword toward the crest of Henry Hill, declared, "Look, men, there is Jackson standing like a stone wall! Let us determine to die here, and we will conquer! Follow me!"[71] The legend of General "Stonewall" Jackson and his "Stonewall" brigade from the valley was born.

Returning to Winchester in command of the Valley District as a major general, Jackson embarked on one of his most heralded campaigns the following spring. Jackson's 1862 Valley Campaign from late March to early June kept occupied and stymied three separate Federal armies that would have otherwise reinforced the forces arrayed against Johnson and, soon after, Robert E. Lee in front of Richmond. It was late June when Lee summoned Jackson's command to the outskirts of Richmond. After a rough start under Lee in repelling McClellan's forces, Jackson began to redeem himself with his ability to conduct independent operations. Lee capitalized on his subordinate's experience by sending his command to Gordonsville in mid-July 1862 to observe the Army of Virginia, the second Federal army that had been assembled in the wake of McClellan's failing Peninsula Campaign. On August 9, Jackson defeated a portion of federal troops of the Army of Virginia at Cedar Mountain, paving the way for Lee's offensive operations that would culminate in the Second Manassas (Second Bull Run) Campaign. Jackson's leadership of the "Left Wing" at Second Manassas and Sharpsburg continued to add fame to the Army of Northern Virginia.

J.E.B. Stuart had earned the praise of both Longstreet and Jackson early in the war. Graduating in the West Point class of 1854, Stuart began his military career as a member of the U.S. Mounted Rifles before transferring to the First U.S. Cavalry, serving primarily on the Kansas frontier for much of the late 1850s under Colonel Edwin V. Sumner, sparring with Native American tribes and quelling disturbances among proslavery and antislavery settlers. (It was these very experiences of Stuart's in the Kansas Territory that helped

Colonel Robert E. Lee identify John Brown in 1859, when the latter took command of U.S. forces and the Virginia militia at Harpers Ferry.) Stuart married the daughter of Colonel Phillip St. George Cooke, who commanded the Second U.S. Dragoons, and later served as a general in the Army of the Potomac, causing a permanent rift in the families—a rift, in fact, that caused Stuart to rename his one-and-a-half-year-old son from Philip St. George Cooke Stuart to James Ewell Brown Stuart Jr. Stuart's loyalty to the Southern cause was in evidence earlier than either Lee, Longstreet or Jackson when he proclaimed at an 1859 oration at Emory and Henry College in Virginia that while the United States was a glorious nation and he loved the Union, "I love *Virginia more*, and if one attachment ever becomes incompatible with the other I scruple not to say '*Virginia* shall command my poor services.'"

Stuart joined the Confederacy in mid-May 1861 after resigning his U.S. Army commission as a captain. Assigned to Colonel Thomas J. Jackson's Harpers Ferry command, Stuart, as a newly minted lieutenant colonel of infantry, was assigned by Jackson to command the cavalry units in his district due to a shortage of posting for cavalry units. This initiated an unlikely but lasting friendship between the two men until death intervened.[72]

Stuart commanded the First Virginia Cavalry at First Manassas and, soon after, the cavalry brigade in the Army of Northern Virginia. During the Peninsula Campaign, Stuart rode around the Army of the

Major General J.E.B. Stuart (1833–1864) commanded the Cavalry Division of the Army of Northern Virginia. Although his horse artillery began the Battle of Fredericksburg, he remained in a minor role. *Valentine Richmond History Center.*

48

Potomac and did so again in the aftermath of Sharpsburg taking his troopers all the way to Chambersburg, Pennsylvania, and back without the loss of a single man. By the late summer of 1862, Stuart's cavalry was a division-sized command, providing Lee with much-needed intelligence of enemy movements and screening the movements of the Confederates from the enemy. Stuart's popularity only increased, as did his daring exploits, leading Lee to declare that his cavalry commander provided "most important and valuable service."[73]

Taking command of the Army of the Potomac in and around Warrenton, Burnside chose to formalize the wing formation that McClellan had devised at Antietam. The army was divided into three "grand divisions" of two corps each. The Right Grand Division comprised the II and IX Corps, the Left Grand Division comprised the I and VI Corps and the Center Grand Division comprised the III and V Corps. Burnside's choice of Major Generals Edwin V. Sumner, William B. Franklin and Joseph Hooker to command these new organizations, respectively, elevated these senior generals into positions where they could easily take command of the army should the Lincoln administration desire to make such subsequent changes. Abolishing the adjutant general's office at his army headquarters, Burnside delegated personnel issues—including transfers, furloughs and leaves of absences—to the three grand division commanders so that he and his staff could focus on the pending campaign. Each grand division also had a cavalry command attached. Brigadier General Alfred Pleasonton commanded the cavalry division assigned to Sumner, while Brigadier Generals George D. Bayard and William W. Averrell commanded cavalry brigades assigned, respectively, to Franklin and Hooker. All of these command changes met with the immediate approval of General Halleck. The Army of the Potomac would muster about 120,000 soldiers for the coming campaign.[74]

On the surface, the creation of grand divisions seemed to be a positive step toward efficiency and the mitigation any hostility among the general officers in the Army of the Potomac who resented the McClellan's removal. Although identified as a loyal McClellanite, Burnside would never measure up to McClellan for some, and he entered army command in an atmosphere of distrust and political intrigue. Militarily, the grand division structure added an additional layer to the standard military chain of command, isolating Burnside from direct control of the various army corps engaged in combat. Unlike Lee, who had maintained a level of professional cohesion among his principal subordinates, Burnside's chief subordinates ran the gambit of political and professional views within the Army of the Potomac that came into conflict. It fell to Burnside as army commander to keep his own subordinates on task to deliver the needed victories for the United States.

Edwin Vose Sumner, commanding Burnside's Right Grand Division, was known as "Bull" due to his booming voice, which could be heard over the roar and din of battle, as well as his sheer stubbornness in battle. "Bull Head," a derivative of his nickname, was used by soldiers behind his back as a result of an Old Army tale that a musket ball at one time glanced off his thick skull. Sumner held the distinction of being the oldest senior commander in the Army of the Potomac and among the oldest generals in the Federal armies.[75]

Born in 1797 and a native of Massachusetts, Sumner was a distant cousin of Charles Sumner, who would become one of the staunchest abolitionists in the U.S. Senate by the time of the Civil War. Enlisting in the army while residing in New York, Sumner was commissioned a second lieutenant in the Second U.S. Infantry in 1819. He served in the Black Hawk War in 1832 and was promoted to captain in the First U.S. Dragoons the following year. While serving at Fort Niagara, New York, at the height of the nullification crisis (when South Carolina threatened to leave the Union over the "tariff of abominations" in 1833), Sumner wrote to his cousin Charles: "If South Carolina stood alone, there would be less cause for apprehension…but is there not every reason to fear that it will result in a controversy between North and South?" Sumner stood ready to assist the federal government if force was needed to compel South Carolina to comply with federal law but hoped that "the difficulty will be quietly and happily adjusted without interruption."[76]

In 1846, Sumner received a promotion to major of the Second U.S. Dragoons and headed to the seat of war in Mexico, earning two brevet promotions for gallantry and meritorious service. At the end of the Mexican-American War, Brevet Colonel Sumner received his promotion as lieutenant colonel of the First Dragoons keeping the peace on the western frontier. He served as military governor of the New Mexico Territory from 1851 to 1853. Appointed colonel of the newly formed First U.S. Cavalry in 1855, Sumner spent much of his time in the Kansas Territory.

It is not clear whether Sumner had been affected by the caning of his kinsman, Senator Charles Sumner, in 1856 by South Carolina congressman Preston Brooks over the senator's statements accusing the southern states of having a prominent role in agitating the violence in "Bleeding Kansas." Commanding a detachment of First Cavalry troopers to dissolve the "free" territorial legislature assembled at Topeka, Colonel Sumner negotiated with armed parties on both sides to disband and disperse their forces. One of the antislavery leaders he dealt with was none other than John Brown, who had given up some proslavery prisoners. Although Brown had federal warrants issued for his arrest, Sumner only took Brown's prisoners and captured arms without making any arrests. Among Sumner's principle officers on this particular mission was Lieutenant J.E.B. Stuart. One Brown biographer has written that Sumner held "mild free-state sympathies" and followed his orders to the narrowest possible definition as to not be accused of proslavery proclivities. This was probably one reason that then secretary of war Jefferson Davis of Mississippi ordered his transfer from Kansas Territory.[77]

Sumner, along with Major David Hunter and Captain John Pope, served as military escorts for president-elect Abraham Lincoln's twelve-day journey from Springfield, Illinois to, Washington, D.C., in early 1861. When reports of possible assassination plots against Lincoln surfaced, his advisors suggested that he take a special evening train from Philadelphia to Baltimore, passing through that city unrecognized and accompanied by a lone bodyguard into Washington. Sumner reportedly called this plan that was ultimately adopted "a d[amne]d piece of cowardice" and recommended a squad of cavalry be ordered to cut a way into the nation's capital. In early 1862, Lincoln appointed Sumner to command the II Corps as part of an early reorganization of McClellan's Army of the Potomac. Sumner fought and received wounds in both the Peninsula Campaign and at Antietam. McClellan had remarked that Sumner had been "a model soldier, but unfortunately nature had limited his capacity to a very narrow extent."[78]

Burnside may have wanted to retain Sumner as his second in command simply because he was not tainted by any cliques or associations among the other general officers within the army. Although the evidence is not entirely clear, Lincoln may have insisted privately that Sumner remain because of his unflinching loyalty to the Union and to the army, bolstering Burnside's own self-confidence. One of the admiring qualities Lincoln found in Burnside was his candor and sincere loyalty to the Union that surpassed his personal friendship and professional confidence in McClellan. At this crucial stage in the war, Lincoln needed all of the loyal generals in the Army of the Potomac that he could muster in carrying out his war aims.

Loyalty to George B. McClellan seemed, on the surface, to be a primary goal for Major General William Buel Franklin, commanding Burnside's Left Grand Division. It had been believed that Franklin was the man to succeed McClellan, given the results of the midterm elections. Born in 1823 the oldest of six children in York, Pennsylvania, Franklin entered West Point at

Major General Edwin V. Sumner (1797–1863), known as "Bull" for his sheer stubbornness, served as Burnside's senior subordinate and commanded the Right Grand Division of the Army of the Potomac comprising the II and IX Corps. *Library of Congress.*

Major General William B. Franklin (1823–1903) commanded the Left Grand Division of the Army of the Potomac comprising the I and VI Corps. He was a brilliant engineer but proved to lack the initiative necessary for a successful battlefield commander. *Library of Congress.*

age nineteen. Graduating at the top of his class, Franklin was assigned to the topographical engineers, an offshoot of the army's corps of engineers responsible for western surveys, navigation-related construction projects and all civil engineering works directed by the United States.[79]

Franklin's early assignments took him on major surveys of the Great Lakes region, a major expedition to the Rocky Mountains and an assignment with the Topographical Bureau in Washington, D.C. Lieutenant Franklin accompanied Brigadier General John E. Wool's march into Mexico at the beginning of the Mexican-American War. Franklin was later brevetted a first lieutenant for gallantry and meritorious service at the Battle of Buena Vista in 1847. Returning to the states, Franklin taught natural and experimental philosophy at his alma mater for three years. He took a leave of absence to supervise surveying and improvement projects along the North Carolina sounds and Oswego Harbor in New York. He also served as an engineer and inspector of lighthouse projects in Maine.

Returning to duty, Franklin became the superintendent of numerous government building projects in Washington, D.C., including the extension of the U.S. Treasury Building, the General Post Office Building and the completion of the U.S. Capitol Building (including the preliminary plans to complete the unfinished dome).[80] At the start of the Civil War, he was a permanent captain in the topographical engineers as a result of fourteen years of service in the army, but he never commanded a significant body of soldiers. This did not hinder War Department officials from appointing Franklin colonel of the Twelfth U.S. Infantry. Three days after this appointment, Colonel Franklin was appointed a brigadier general of volunteers and commanded a brigade at First Bull Run. In less than a year, Franklin went from brigade to division to corps command at the start of the Peninsula Campaign, commanding the VI Corps. His performances on the Peninsula and at Antietam were lackluster, demonstrating that the meticulous skills necessary for great engineers were not traits needed to enhance flexibility, versatility and resourcefulness essential for seasoned field commanders.[81]

Franklin, perhaps undeservedly, received the wrath of John Pope in his failed Second Bull Run Campaign, along with then V Corps commander Fitz-John Porter, for deliberately ensuring the defeat of his Army of Virginia by failing to provide needed reinforcements from the Army of the Potomac. Franklin escaped formal censure, but Porter was removed from command and subsequently dismissed from the army after a court-martial, serving as a scapegoat for the failed campaign. Franklin found that he needed to be on his own guard once McClellan was removed.[82]

Franklin, like McClellan, believed that emancipation should have no bearing on the war's aims. He also shared with Burnside an extreme dislike of Joseph Hooker. At the moment, Burnside was the "the only one who could have been chosen with whom things would have gone on so quietly," as Franklin confided to his wife a week after McClellan's replacement.[83]

If the general officers of the Army of the Potomac were divided between those who liked McClellan and those who did not, "Fighting Joe" Hooker became the self-appointed leader of the latter group. Joseph Hooker, commanding Burnside's Center Grand Division, hated his nickname, attributed to a reporter's typographical error. "People will think I am a highwayman or a bandit," Hooker said as he recalled his initial reaction to the popular epitaph.[84] He no doubt proved himself an aggressive division and corps commander in the Army of the Potomac, dearly loved by the rank and file. Born in 1814 in Hadley, Massachusetts, Hooker was a grandson and namesake of a veteran captain of the American Revolution. As a member of the West Point class of 1837, Hooker was among the outspoken cadets representing the antislavery position of the northern section of the country.[85] He found himself in a fistfight with his southern classmate, Jubal A. Early of Virginia, after a debating society meeting in which he "made a scurrilous attack on the slaveholders of the South." Early apparently emerged victorious in their subsequent fight, as he was very well satisfied over the final outcome of their quarrel.[86]

After graduating from West Point, Lieutenant Hooker was assigned to the First U.S. Artillery and sent to the continuing war against the Seminoles in Florida. He later served in Tennessee as part of the military force corralling resistant Cherokees in preparation for their relocation west. Hooker briefly served as post adjutant at West Point before being appointed regimental adjutant for the First Artillery, with its headquarters stationed in Maine. It was during this time that an observer considered him "one of the handsomest men in the Army."[87]

Hooker served on the staff of five different generals commanding volunteer troops during the Mexican-American War. His regular army experience compensated for shortcomings of these volunteer generals. One general remarked that Hooker's "coolness and self-possession in battle set an example to both officers and men that exerted a most happy influence." Another general, Gideon J. Pillow, under whom Hooker served, told him pointedly, "When you see occasion for issuing an order, give it without reference to me. You understand these matters." It would be Hooker's later testimony on behalf of General Pillow during the latter's court-martial that earned Hooker enmity from General Winfield Scott for years to come.[88]

Hooker returned to the states as a brevet lieutenant colonel. Although retaining his rank as a captain, he was soon after appointed assistant adjutant general of the Pacific Division, based in Sonoma, California. He resigned from the army in 1853. When the Civil War began, Hooker offered his services to the United States, seeking a commission. Due to General Scott's ill feelings toward Hooker for the past thirteen years, he was ignored. Hooker arrived in Washington in time to witness, as a civilian observer, the Federal disaster at First Bull Run.[89] Later presented to President Lincoln on a visit to the White House as "Captain Hooker," he promptly corrected the chief executive:

> *Mr. President, I was introduced to you as Captain Hooker. I am, or was, Lieutenant Colonel Hooker of the Regular Army. When this war broke out I was at home in California, and hastened to make a tender of my services to the Government; but my relation to General Scott, or some other impediment, stands in the way, and I now see no chance of making my military knowledge and experience useful. I am about to return, but before going I was anxious to pay my respects to you, Sir, and to express my wish for your personal welfare, and for your success in putting down the rebellion. And while I am about it, Mr. President, I want to say one thing more, and that is, that I was at the battle of Bull Run the other day, and it is neither vanity nor boasting in me to declare that I am a damned sight better General than you, Sir, had on that field.*

Lincoln, impressed with the boldness of the veteran officer before him, offered him a colonel's commission and command of a regiment. Soon after, he was commissioned a brigadier general of volunteers.[90]

Hooker had truly earned his nickname during the Peninsula Campaign, Second Bull Run and Antietam. Nevertheless, his insatiable ambition and dissatisfaction with McClellan and his supporters in the Army of the Potomac caused Hooker to become openly critical of his military superiors and the Lincoln administration among influential Washington circles and in the press. Given his apparently antislavery views, Hooker had cultivated a political following among the radical wing of Republicans while recuperating from his Antietam wound. Many clamored for his appointment to command the Army of the Potomac, but Burnside had proven to be Lincoln's choice.

Lincoln, possessing very little military experience but maintaining a healthy dose of common sense, had urged McClellan in mid-October to

Major General Joseph Hooker (1814–1879) commanded the Center Grand Division of the Army of the Potomac comprising the III and V Corps. Possessing the best combat record of all grand division commanders, "Fighting Joe" held designs to gain command of the Army of the Potomac. *National Archives.*

maintain the "inside track" in a movement toward Richmond that would force Lee into a decisive battle. "We should not so operate as to merely drive him away," the president reminded McClellan. "As we must beat him somewhere, or fail finally." Burnside, upon assuming command, decided to abandon his predecessor's apparent advance along the Orange and Alexandria Railroad toward Gordonsville and switch his operations eastward along the Richmond, Fredericksburg and Potomac Railroad, with Fredericksburg serving as a base of operations. He explained his rationale to the War Department:

In moving by way of Fredericksburg there is no point up to the time when we should reach that place at which we will not be nearer to Washington than the enemy, and we will all the time be on the shortest route to Richmond, the taking of which, I think, should be the great object of the campaign, as the fall of that place would tend more to cripple the rebel cause than almost any other military event, except the absolute breaking up of their army...A great reason for feeling that the Fredericksburg route is the best, is that if we are detained by the elements, it would be much better for us to be on that route.[91]

Burnside recalled offering McClellan his opinion "that if he [McClellan] proposed to go to Richmond by land, he would have to go by way of Fredericksburg; and in that he partially agreed with me." Sometime later, a similar conversation occurred with several other officers present. A day before his removal, McClellan had ordered all available pontoon bridges in

Berlin, Maryland, to be sent to Washington "in case he decided to go by way of Fredericksburg," according to Burnside.[92]

On November 12, Halleck, accompanied by Montgomery C. Meigs, the army's chief quartermaster, and Herman Haupt, superintendent of the military railroad, met with Burnside at his headquarters in Warrenton. Burnside reiterated his belief that he was unfit for army command, which Halleck quickly dispelled. Although Halleck hoped to convince the new army commander to follow the president's plan of operating along the Orange and Alexandria Railroad, Burnside insisted on his proposed plan to shift his operations to Fredericksburg. To Halleck's chagrin, Haupt endorsed Burnside, arguing that the Army of the Potomac could be sustained by undisturbed water supply lines once the destroyed wharves at both Aquia Landing and Belle Plain on the Potomac River were rebuilt. Moreover, it would take less time to repair the Richmond, Fredericksburg and Potomac Railroad than the Orange and Alexandria, and the former route was much easier to protect.

Declining to overrule Burnside as he had the discretion to do as general in chief, Halleck returned to Washington to confer with Lincoln. Telegraphing Burnside two days later, Halleck reported Lincoln's approval. "He thinks it will succeed, if you move very rapidly," Halleck cautioned, "otherwise not." On that same day, Halleck ordered the volunteer engineer brigade under Brigadier General Daniel P. Woodbury stationed in Washington to be ready for detached service, presumably with the Army of the Potomac. McClellan's original order for the pontoon bridges in Maryland to be moved to Washington had been received by the officer commanding them six days after the date of the order. It was only due to the diligence of Lieutenant Cyrus B. Comstock, Burnside's chief engineer, upon his chief's insistence, who had discovered that the pontoons had received their orders later than expected.[93]

Meanwhile, Burnside had put his army in motion on November 15. Executing a feint from Warrenton on a broad front in the direction of Culpeper with some elements of the Army of the Potomac, Burnside followed Lincoln's directive in rapidly shifting his army east, leaving Lee's Confederates unsure of Federal intentions.[94]

Lee, writing to President Davis two days later, was doubtful that Burnside's destination was Fredericksburg, as there was no indication that the wharf at Aquia Landing had been rebuilt "for subsisting a large army." Observing that rail cars were active on the Orange and Alexandria line, the Confederate commander could not "tell whether they [Federals] are carrying back or bringing forward troops." As a precaution, Lee ordered the small Confederate force that amounted to no more than 1,500 at Fredericksburg to destroy the

Burnside and his staff at Warrenton, Virginia, shortly after assuming command of the Army of the Potomac. *Library of Congress.*

tracks of the Richmond, Fredericksburg and Potomac Railroad north of the Rappahannock, as well as destroy the remaining bridges in the vicinity of the city.[95]

Sumner's Right Grand Division made a rapid march to Falmouth, arriving on November 17 just opposite Fredericksburg. Hooker's Center Grand Division, following Sumner's route the next day, halted at Hartwood Church six miles northwest of Falmouth, while Franklin's Left Grand Division marched to Stafford Courthouse about ten miles to the northeast of Falmouth.

The Army of the Potomac's initial objective was in easy reach when Burnside was informed that the pontoon bridges needed to cross the Rappahannock had just received orders to move from Washington that same day, delaying his planned operations. Portions of the Federal II Corps in Sumner's Grand Division silenced four Confederate artillery cannons positioned just across the river. Sumner asked Burnside for permission to cross at a shallow ford above Falmouth and occupy lightly defended Fredericksburg. Fearing the possibility of having a portion of his army isolated in enemy territory before the rest of his army arrived and his supply bases secured, Burnside wisely ordered Sumner to stay put. Within a short time, heavy rains caused

Confederate soldiers (possibly Mississippians of Barksdale's Brigade) "posing" in
Fredericksburg for a photographer on the other side of the damaged bridge—taken some
time in early 1863 after the battle. *National Archives.*

the fords of the Rappahannock to become impassable. Agreeing with his
commander's rationale, the old soldier Sumner still believed that crossing
the river would be of paramount importance. "I knew that neither our
government nor our people would be satisfied to have our entire army retire
from this position, or go into winter quarters, until we knew the force that
was on the other side of the river; and they only way in which we could learn
that was by going over there and feeling of them."[96]

This proved to be a critical moment in the campaign for Burnside.
Should he wait until the pontoons arrived to cross his army in the vicinity of
Fredericksburg? Should he shift his base of operations elsewhere—presumably
to southeastern Virginia—and advance toward Richmond along the James
River or pursue a modified advance against the divided Army of Northern
Virginia that Lincoln and Halleck had advocated previously? Burnside chose
to wait.

As late as November 19, Robert E. Lee remained in the dark over the
true intentions of Burnside. Although recent reports had indicated Sumner's

arrival at Falmouth, the Confederate commander was not ultimately convinced that Fredericksburg was the Federal destination, as he wrote to Jackson while still in the Shenandoah Valley, "I do not now anticipate making a stand north of the North Anna." The North Anna River, almost twenty-five miles south of Fredericksburg, was where Lee believed he could best mount a stout defense barring the Army of the Potomac from Richmond.[97]

In order to buy time for an anticipated defense along the North Anna, Lee had already given Longstreet's Corps at Culpeper its marching orders the previous day for movement to the southeast. McLaws's Division moved to Fredericksburg, while Ransom's Division headed for Hanover Junction, where the Richmond, Fredericksburg and Potomac Railroad met the Virginia Central Railroad. Ransom's men were later redirected to Guiney's Station just south of Fredericksburg in support of McLaws. Anderson's Division marched for Spotsylvania Courthouse, while Hood's and Pickett's divisions headed toward the North Anna. Jackson, at his discretion, could remain in the Valley, taking every opportunity that "cripples and embarrasses the general movement of the enemy" but remaining free to unite with Longstreet's Corps in the event of a battle.

Upon receiving intelligence that Burnside's Federals had not crossed the Rappahannock, Lee ordered all of Longstreet's units to Fredericksburg. For the moment, Fredericksburg and the Rappahannock River would be obstacles to slow the enemy's movements, as Lee sought to unite his separated corps to protect the Confederate capital and, ultimately, the Confederate cause.[98]

Chapter 3

Fredericksburg

Right in the Wrong Place

Fredericksburg is right in the wrong place," Confederate president Jefferson Davis remarked to General Joseph E. Johnston on an impromptu reconnaissance of the area in mid-March 1862. Johnston commanded the expansive Department of Northern Virginia for the Confederate military. Observing Fredericksburg from across the Rappahannock in Falmouth, Davis expressed the vulnerability of the town should Federal forces occupy the heights on their side of the river. The only adequate defense on the opposite side was the high ground located behind Fredericksburg, surrounding as if it were at the bottom of an amphitheatre. Disappointed at Johnson's recent withdrawal of Confederate troops from Centreville and Manassas all the way to the south side of the Rappahannock, Davis did not want to relinquish any more territory to the Federals than necessary.[99]

Lee, at this time, served as Davis's military advisor and nominal general in chief (essentially Halleck's role in the Federal armies). As Federal forces advanced toward Fredericksburg, Lee counseled Major General Theophilus Holmes commanding the Aquia District (which included Fredericksburg) to not give up his position on the Rappahannock nor the supply depot at Fredericksburg. "It is not the plan of the [Confederate] Government to abandon any country that can be held, and it is only the necessity of the case, I presume, that has caused the withdrawal of the troops to the Rappahannock," Lee wrote, echoing Davis's sentiments to Holmes's immediate superior, Johnston. "I trust there will be no necessity of retrograding farther."[100]

Above: A view of
Fredericksburg from
the eastern bank of the
Rappahannock River,
looking northwest.
Marye's Heights is the
high ground in the left
center. *Library of Congress.*

Left: Jefferson Davis
(1808–1889), former
U.S. senator from
Mississippi and
president of the
Confederate States of
America. He believed
that the town of
Fredericksburg was
"right in the wrong
place." *Library of
Congress.*

Fredericksburg

Johnston had already ordered his subordinate commanders to abandon their positions north of the Rappahannock, including the Fredericksburg depot. Holmes, apparently not having heard from Johnston, sent a frantic note of appeal to Lee in Richmond on March 16:

> *If the town* [Fredericksburg] *is abandoned you may expect an utter demoralization of the people, which I greatly fear will be reflected on the troops. These at present are in a high state of discipline and are most anxious to meet the enemy, but they are not veterans and cannot be relied on in a retreat. The object of the enemy is certainly an immediate advance on Richmond, and this is certainly their most direct and available route, and it will be a thousand times better for us to concentrate there at once and be prepared to meet them in a general engagement than to be separated as we are, and liable to be beaten and demoralized in detail. The idea of deserting this noble and generous people grieves my heart beyond measure, and I am perfectly willing to sacrifice myself and every soldier that I have to protect them…it is for you, my dear general, who have all the lights, before you, to say whether we shall fight the enemy.*

Lee expressed his regret to Holmes that he and other officers believed that Fredericksburg was in an untenable situation. Recommending an alternative location of a supply depot near Hanover Junction, Lee hoped that the Rappahannock line could be maintained. Writing to Johnston, Lee reiterated Holmes's concerns about abandoning Fredericksburg. "From what is stated of the conditions of the roads," Lee concluded, "I hardly think an immediate movement [by the Federals] against Fredericksburg can be made." Lee, not wishing to supersede the orders of Johnston as an army field commander, closed his letter by acknowledging to his West Point classmate that "[y]ou have doubtless considered the subject with reference to your operations, and made your arrangements as to the points to be held and defended." One month later, Major General Irvin McDowell's Federal soldiers entered Falmouth and would soon occupy Fredericksburg as part of the Department of the Rappahannock in the Federal military.[101]

Lee may have experienced a brief touch of déjà vu seven months later as his Confederate legions began entering Fredericksburg on the evening of November 20, 1862. His role as an army commander was much different than as general in chief coordinating the military operations for the overall Confederate war effort. Lee believed that very little could be done to prevent Federal forces from crossing the Rappahannock in the vicinity of Fredericksburg. This was the same problem that had confronted the Confederate military leadership earlier that year. Lee preferred falling back to the North Anna River for the best defense of Richmond, as well as protecting the Army of Northern Virginia from unnecessary casualties while in a defensive posture. "My purpose was changed not from any advantage in this position," Lee later wrote reiterating his view of the broader Confederate war effort, "but from an unwillingness to open more of our country to depredation than possible." He also hoped to collect much-needed supplies and provisions in the Rappahannock River Valley.[102]

The "noble and generous people" of Fredericksburg rejoiced when the veteran South Carolinians, Georgians and Mississippians of Lafayette McLaws's division entered their town, soon followed by the makeshift division composed exclusively of North Carolinians under Robert Ransom Jr. "We were greatly surprised, but equally delighted, to find we were to be defended," said Matilda Hamilton, who resided at Forest Hill, "and that dear Fredericksburg was not again to be given up to the Yankees."[103]

Fredericksburg, named in 1728 in honor of Prince Frederick of Wales, who would never live to become the English monarch, was located at the falls of the Rappahannock River. Until the nineteenth century, Fredericksburg served as an important colonial commercial and trading center and was the farthest point inland that oceangoing vessels could reach in early Virginia.[104] As the decades of the early nineteenth century progressed, Fredericksburg fell behind in commercial importance to other Virginia locales. Economic revitalization came on the eve of the Civil War through the construction of a dam and alterations to an existing canal that maintained agricultural productivity in grain staples while fostering

Another view of Fredericksburg from the eastern bank of the Rappahannock River, looking southwest. Note the steeples of both the Episcopal and Baptist churches to the far left. The circuit courthouse between the two churches is obscured by the tree on this side of the river. *Library of Congress.*

several mills and factories. In spite of fluctuations in Fredericksburg's antebellum economy, the institution of slavery continued to be an integral part in economic life and the social order.[105]

Fredericksburg and its environs provided glimpses into the various strata of slave society in Virginia. South of town, in neighboring Spotsylvania County, large numbers of slaves labored on plantations and larger farms, which would form the typical view of the Old South. North of the Rappahannock in Stafford County, slaves resided and worked on smaller landholdings often working alongside their white owners. Fredericksburg itself represented a glimpse into urban slavery where skilled slaves hired out their time or were domestic servants to the town dwellers. Fredericksburg ranked seventh behind Winchester in the Shenandoah Valley for the largest number of free African Americans in 1860. Members of this particular group had often accumulated property and operated business before the war but stood to lose a great deal, even their own freedom, if they stepped out of line.[106]

Slavery proved a complex institution that involved human relationships with slaves having experiences that ran the gambit of dealing with cruel tyrants for masters to benevolent owners with affectionate concern for their welfare. The *Fredericksburg News* reported in 1861, "We hear that the Negroes of Fredericksburg are trying to organize a company for the old Town." Confederate forces apparently never used this company as a combat unit. It was also reported that free black residents of Spotsylvania County had placed their labors and property at Virginia's disposal after the state joined the Confederacy. At least twenty-eight of these sable residents were employed in transporting ammunition to various Confederate posts in northern Virginia.[107]

If African Americans in the Fredericksburg area had provided support to the Confederacy through their voluntary efforts or coercion, the arrival of General McDowell's Federal command began to tip the scale in favor of the Union, whether white Northerners intended to become "Yankee abolitionists" or not. One Federal officer serving in the Shenandoah Valley near Harrisonburg in late April 1862 made a general observation of Virginia slaves in a letter to his daughter:

The Negro population increases as we go south, and although they all understand that the rear is open to them, very few leave their masters. Indeed many of them are afraid at first, probably from big stories of our cruelties that told them. They seem glad at our coming and probably think some great benefit is to accrue to them, but they show very little desire to quit their present homes. In truth they are much attached to their localities, and but for the fear of being sold south I don't think a dozen could be coaxed away. As it is, probably fifty have come in and are employed by our quartermasters. If the abolitionists could see things as they really are here they would have less confidence in the aid of the Negro.

Another Federal officer from Wisconsin camped near Fredericksburg had a different experience that countered this view:

Our camps are now flooded with negroes, with packs on their backs, and bound for freedom. No system of abolition could have swept the system away more effectually than does the advance of our army…with the sympathy and active assistance of the soldiers, the poor slaves were breaking their fetters in spite of their masters…the slave made good his title to liberty, by taking refuge with the soldiers.[108]

John M. Washington, a young slave, was owned by Thomas Ware, a former purser in the U.S. Navy who had joined the Confederate navy. Washington had been hired out to work as a dining room steward and barkeeper at the Shakespeare House Hotel in Fredericksburg when Federal troops first occupied Falmouth that spring. The hotel proprietors, who were serving as officers in the Thirtieth Virginia Infantry, had given Washington a roll of bills to pay the other hotel servants and secure the hotel building and property as the Confederates evacuated Fredericksburg. It was anticipated that Washington would serve as a personal servant in a Confederate unit bound for North Carolina. Performing his requested tasks and returning the hotel keys to the wife of the hotel's proprietor, Washington crossed in a boat provided by Federal soldiers on the other side and was welcomed into Federal lines when he reached the shore, where he distributed "rebel newspapers" he had stuffed in his pockets to his new friends. Eventually, he would become a servant to the headquarters staff of Brigadier General Rufus R. King. He recollected his first day of freedom years later:

Before morning I had began to fee[l] like I had truly Escaped from the hand of the slaves master and with the help of God, I never would be a slave no more. I felt for the first time in my life that I could now claim Every cent that I should work for as my own. I began now to feel that life had a new joy awaiting me. I might now go and come as I Pleased so I wood [sic] remain with the army until I got Enough money to travel further North…

Fredericksburg

Hundreds of colord [sic] *people obtained passes and free transportation to Washington and the North. And made their Escape to the <u>Free States</u>.*

Aquia Landing—the northern terminus of the Richmond, Fredericksburg and Potomac Railroad and located on Aquia Creek, which emptied into the Potomac River—served as a wharf for both Confederate and Federal forces during the first half of the war. At least ten thousand slaves reached this point during the war on their way to Washington, D.C., and points north.[109] Ambrose Burnside, attempting to venture farther south, was stalled for the lack of pontoon bridges. Meeting with Sumner and the army's provost marshal, Brigadier General Marsena R. Patrick, Burnside decided to demand the surrender of Fredericksburg. Patrick, who had commanded a brigade at Fredericksburg the previous spring and had gained a favorable reputation with the residents, received the mission of delivering the ultimatum composed by Sumner under Burnside's direction to city officials on the morning of November 21. Citing military protocol at the Federal general's initial encounter with enemy pickets, the Confederate garrison

Chatham Manor (Lacy House) was officially Sumner's headquarters at Fredericksburg but also served as a gathering point for the Federal high command on several occasions during the campaign. It also functioned as a signal station, a staging area for Federal engineers building the pontoon bridges and a hospital for Federals wounded in action against Marye's Heights. *Library of Congress.*

commander who held Fredericksburg prior to the arrival of Lee's advance units sent a courier to his military superiors.

Sumner's ultimatum letter intended for Mayor Montgomery Slaughter and the Fredericksburg Common Council made a detour to Robert E. Lee's headquarters tent, where Generals Longstreet and McLaws had joined their chief. Sumner charged Confederate troops with firing on his command from across the river from the cover of city dwellings and argued that the mills, factories and railroad continued to support those in rebellion against the United States. As a result, Fredericksburg would have to surrender by 5:00 p.m. that day. Failing to do so, Sumner would "proceed to shell the town" after a sixteen-hour period, which would allow for the removal of women and children as well as wounded and sick enemy soldiers.

Lee dispatched two general officers to meet with Mayor Slaughter and members of the city council, assuring them that their commander "would not occupy or use the city for military purposes, but…would resist its occupation by the enemy." Meanwhile, Longstreet sent his chief of staff, Major G. Moxley Sorrell, to Patrick, who had been waiting more than three hours for a response, making it unmistakably clear that the Army of Northern Virginia had arrived at Fredericksburg.

After convening an emergency city council meeting, Mayor Slaughter and a delegation met with Patrick later that evening conveying Lee's position that the Confederates would not occupy the town for military purposes "and that the condition of things therein complained of shall no longer exist." Burnside and his subordinates knew such assurances rang hollow when Patrick returned from his mission. As historian Frank O'Reilly has written, "The contending armies placed the population of Fredericksburg in an ambiguous and frightening predicament." Neither army occupied the town, as Burnside lacked the means of crossing the Rappahannock and Lee withdrew Longstreet's Corps into positions on the hills over a mile west and south of the city. The specter of being shelled prompted Slaughter and a delegation of Confederate generals to meet with General Patrick the following day; it was resolved that Fredericksburg would not be shelled as long as the residents did not consent to Confederate forces using their city to shell Federal forces first.[110]

A tenuous truce notwithstanding, Fredericksburg residents had begun their exodus to points farther south. Residents with some means took available rail cars to Richmond with their valuables, including slaves, in tow. Within a day of the arrival of both armies, Federal artillery mistakenly fired on a trainload of fleeing residents bound for Richmond "supposing

Fredericksburg

Princess Anne Street was a major thoroughfare through Fredericksburg that ran north to south. It contained several local government buildings and houses of worship, including the circuit courthouse in the foreground and Episcopal church behind. *Library of Congress.*

the cars (baggage) conveying military stores," according to a civilian in the Confederate capital. Luckily for the passengers, the shell missed its intended target and the firing ceased, with apologies coming from Federal military authorities.[111]

Other residents sought refuge out in the immediate countryside if not on the homesteads in neighboring Spotsylvania and Orange Counties in the open air of the surrounding woods. William Stilwell of the Fifty-third Georgia was ordered by his brigade commander, Brigadier General Paul Semmes, to accompany a guard and wagon to assist in the evacuation of Fredericksburg's residents wishing to seek safety. Stilwell wrote to his wife:

I was so sorry for the poor little innocent children and the ladies seemed to be scared out of anything like reason, but I told them I had heard bigger dogs bark than that and never been bit yet. They would then cry and scold the Yankees... To see from the little child that could just walk to the mother of seventy years old with her cane trying to walk through the muddy streets with loads of baggage presented a sight not pleasant to look on.

At the time of truce negotiations between the Federal high command and Fredericksburg officials, Jackson's Second Corps of the Army of Northern Virginia had left Virginia's Shenandoah Valley and was making its way south to join Lee and Longstreet.[112]

The arrival of the bulk of Jackson's men at Fredericksburg by December 3 enabled the Army of Northern Virginia to defend a thirty-two-mile front south of the Rappahannock River. Longstreet's forty-thousand-man force anchored its left flank in fortified positions near Banks Ford slightly more than three miles above Fredericksburg. The Confederate line continued for seven miles in a southeasterly fashion, occupying Marye's Heights behind the city and the high ground known as Spotsylvania Heights parallel to the Richmond, Fredericksburg and Potomac Railroad. Near Hamilton's Crossing, where the railroad intersected with the Mine Road below the city, Longstreet's line linked with Jackson's thirty-eight thousand unfortified troops, stretching for an additional twenty miles to the small town of Port Royal in neighboring Caroline County.[113]

Burnside lost the element of surprise, as evident by the presence of Lee's entire army across the river. His ability to cross the Rappahannock would not go uncontested now, even when the lead elements of his missing pontoon bridge trains manned by the Fiftieth New York Engineers arrived at his headquarters on November 25 amid a heavy downpour. The nineteen-day delay from McClellan's original orders stemmed from a combination of miscommunication among higher authorities and the engineer units, lack of follow-up by the various military bureaus and poor weather. Private Josiah F. Murphey of the Twentieth Massachusetts provided a simple description of the pontoon bridges that were once to be a saving grace for Burnside but were now the bane of his tenure so far in command of the army:

It is a floating bridge made of square end boats that we would term scows, anchored at both ends, headed up and down stream about 10 or 15 feet apart. Timbers fitted for the purpose are place across them from boat to boat and planking laid across the timber another set of timber laid over the planking to keep them in place. It makes a good bridge over which artillery, infantry and cavalry can pass in safty [sic]. Our trouble now [was] to get a bridge across the river to which the rebs objected very decidedly.[114]

Fredericksburg

As Burnside pondered his next move, Federal and Confederate soldiers settled into a comfortable routine of picket duty along the river's edge. Upon the Army of the Potomac's first arrival, "hundreds of the rebels and our men lined the banks of the river in our front, and indulged in spicy repartee and generally good-natured defiance across the narrow river which divided us (about two hundred yards wide)" by sunset, according to Charles Walcott of the Twenty-first Massachusetts Infantry. A member of the Eighteenth Mississippi Infantry, finding the opposing sides becoming "very friendly," recalled:

> *The Confederates would send tobacco in little bark boats over to the "Yanks," and the latter would send us back coffee and other articles. It finally got so that the pickets would not shoot at each other. The men became very expert in setting the sails on the bark, which they could land at almost the very place they selected for the exchange of commodities. It was a strange sight to watch the men of opposing armies playing and trafficking as if there was no war, but they were ready to face each at any minute, and fight like lions and tigers if the orders were given.*[115]

One soldier in the Seventh Rhode Island Infantry was the recipient of "spicy repartee" and "defiance" when he saw "[o]ne reb in a blue coat surprised his Yankee neighbors when he inquired where his commissary and his quartermaster were now (referring to Generals Pope and McDowell)." The riverbank became the popular spot for the exchange of "witty remarks," some of an "uncomplimentary character." Confederate soldiers were often anxious to obtain Northern papers for Richmond papers, in addition to the illicit exchange of contraband articles, usually in the form of tobacco and coffee.[116]

In spite of the "friendly" atmosphere, Federal officers kept on their guard when inspecting their picket posts. Captain James Wren of the Forty-eighth Pennsylvania observed that "[t]he rebel pickets eyed me very sharp with a spy glass. I being mounted." Confederate soldiers knew about Burnside's replacement of McClellan in command of the Army of the Potomac within a day that it was announced to Federal soldiers, and their ability to obtain other important military information kept their adversaries on their toes. The commanding officer of a New York artillery battery, given orders along with the rest of the army to issue three days' rations, realized that "the rebels well knew that that meant a fight or a march. I think every rebel knew of this issue."[117]

A sketch of Federal pickets examining passes near the Rappahannock. *Lumley, Library of Congress.*

Another sketch of Federal pickets across from Fredericksburg. *Waud, Library of Congress.*

The lack of movement on Burnside's part prompted President Lincoln to make a brief visit to Burnside on board the steamer *Baltimore* anchored in the middle of Aquia Creek on the evening of November 27.[118] Burnside shared his frustrations over the delay of the pontoon bridges and pressure that he believed was coming from Halleck. Lincoln assured his general that it was the president who held overall authority for military operations and that he should conduct operations when he felt ready of success. Halleck had already shown his penchant for passing the mantel of responsibility onto the shoulders of others; he acknowledged that he promised to render all the assistance he could in his power but that all orders, policies and requisitions with regard to the Army of the Potomac rested with Burnside. "I told [Burnside] not to send me any requisitions," he explained, "but to make them on the proper heads of departments." When Burnside complained to the War Department over the pontoon delays, Halleck told him "to arrest any person who had neglected his duty." When asked by members of the Joint Committee on the Conduct of the War immediately following the Battle of Fredericksburg, Joseph Hooker, who was a rival for command of the army, admitted that he believed that the responsibility for ensuring that the pontoon bridges and supplies arrived with the army "rested upon General Halleck and General Meigs, because it was beyond the control of General Burnside, who was not where he could control it."[119]

Likewise, Halleck deferred making judgments on the plans of field commanders until he consulted and received approval from the president. Lincoln's patience would reach the critical point with Halleck's inability to issue definitive orders to subordinate generals. This was precisely what he and Secretary Stanton had appointed him to do in the first place as general in chief. "Your military skill is useless to me if you will not do this," Lincoln wrote later to Halleck. General Haupt, defending Halleck from charges of meddling in Burnside's military operations, as critics had charged civilian authorities, argued after the war that Halleck's usual method would be to "indicate to the commander of an army the objects to be accomplished, but would leave him untrammeled as far as details were concerned." It became all too clear that Burnside needed guidance from someone with sound military experience and judgment, but Halleck did not fit the bill.[120]

Burnside and Lincoln discussed the three main options for the coming campaign: crossing directly in front of Fredericksburg; crossing above Fredericksburg to turn Lee's left; or crossing below Fredericksburg to turn Lee's right. An attempted crossing at Fredericksburg in front of Lee's army when the enemy's strength remained uncertain was something Lincoln did not wish to entertain. He wanted Burnside's operations to be free from as much risk as possible. Sumner, who had wanted to seize Fredericksburg on his first arrival, later lamented that had the pontoons been in place at that time, his grand division could have "crossed the heights in rear of Fredericksburg before the enemy could reach them." Even if Lee had beaten the Army of the Potomac to Richmond, the Federals still would have had the railroad in their position, preventing the erection of fortifications, Sumner surmised.[121] Sumner would have a change of view when it was clear that a sizable Confederate force occupied the heights behind Fredericksburg. He cautioned Burnside that crossing "over to the town might be attended with great loss, not only from their artillery, but every house within musket range could be filled with Infantry."[122]

Hooker became the leading advocate for crossing above Fredericksburg. On November 19, when his grand division first arrived in bivouac near Hartwood Church, "Fighting Joe" had recommended to Burnside that he could cross his troops near Richard's Ford with three days' rations, advance on Bowling Green or Sexton's Junction and turn Lee's left. Burnside pointed out that Sexton's Junction would separate him from the rest of the army by thirty-six miles and that the farther north he ventured from his position, he would encounter not only the Rappahannock River but also the Rapidan River. Since rain had been present at a steady pace for some time, fording two rivers would make the ability to reinforce and resupply Hooker's men virtually impossible. Mindful that Hooker possibly had some underlying motive to make such a suggestion in some complex scheme to undermine his command authority, Burnside politely thanked him as he was "always very glad to take advice of my general officers, and should always be loth [sic] to make a move without consulting them." According to Burnside, Hooker replied with gratitude for considering his proposal and agreed that the weather made it difficult to undertake.

If Burnside had held any intimation that Hooker had underlying motives for making his proposal, they would prove correct. Hooker, on the same day he wrote to Burnside, wrote directly to Secretary Stanton outlining the same proposal. Only this time, poor weather did not seem to pose a problem to his plans; "[t]he lateness of the season demands unusual vigor in the prosecution of the campaign," Hooker wrote, in a veiled attempt to discredit Burnside. Eager to elevate his own fitness to command the army, Hooker concluded, "I regret that the major-general commanding did not keep up a show of an advance on the line via Gordonsville, and even now I would recommend a demonstration, with a strong infantry force and cavalry force, in that direction."[123] Hooker was the lone objector in a December 3 meeting with Burnside and the grand division commanders, where he upheld "my preference that the whole army should cross at what is called the United States or Richard's Ford" twelve miles above Fredericksburg. Burnside, Sumner and Franklin had settled already on operations below Fredericksburg.[124]

Lincoln had expressed his preference for turning Lee's right below Fredericksburg at some point in his meeting with Burnside on board the

Baltimore and perhaps as well in a subsequent meeting in Washington a day or two later. Specifically, Lincoln hoped that Burnside would consider crossing troops at Skinker's Neck, a massive bend in the Rappahannock about twelve miles below Fredericksburg, while the rest of the Army of the Potomac crossed in the vicinity of Fredericksburg. He also hoped that another Federal force could operate farther south along the Pamunkey River, where Lee would not be able to fall back on Richmond. Burnside believed that opening a second front on the Pamunkey would take too much time but already had cavalry patrols and engineers inspecting Skinker's Neck for crossing troops in a diversionary movement to force the Confederates to shift troops south from Fredericksburg and weaken the defenses behind the town. By the December 3 meeting, Burnside had his operational plan. Sumner later commented, "[A]fter the preparations were made to cross at Skinker's Neck, after a large number of wagons had been sent by the general down there in order to deceive the enemy, I was decidedly in favor of throwing the bridges over here [Fredericksburg] and carrying the town…as the enemy were marching their troops down below expecting that we were going to cross down there." Burnside soon realized that plans can go awry, especially when the element of surprise was lost.[125]

Four U.S. Navy gunboats of the Potomac Flotilla ventured upriver on December 4 in support of a crossing of Burnside's army at Skinker's Neck. The naval squadron encountered enemy artillery fire below Port Royal from Stuart's Horse Artillery under the command of Major John Pelham. As the gunboats continued upriver, they met the guns of the Rockbridge

Burnside explored the possibility of operating against the Confederate right at Skinker's Neck (sketched here), several miles to the southeast of Fredericksburg, but the Rappahannock proved too wide and deep for effective military operations. *Waud, Library of Congress.*

Artillery and, near a place called Pratt's Landing, were fired upon by artillery batteries of D.H. Hill's Confederate division of Jackson's Corps. Unable to proceed farther without incurring serious damage to the vessels or tallying casualties, the squadron fell back out of the range of the land-based artillery, with Pelham's horse artillery giving "them a parting shot." D.H. Hill later reported that these Federal "pirates" had "partially destroyed [Port Royal], but a merciful God kindly protected the inoffensive inhabitants. A dog was killed and a negro wounded; no other living being was injured." Not only was Skinker's Neck off the table with regard to Burnside's offensive operations, but the presence of D.H. Hill's division was also a clear indicator that Jackson had arrived and prepared to meet their enemy in that quarter.[126]

Jackson's columns had first arrived in Fredericksburg on December 1 and had begun manning positions farther south to Port Royal for the next two days. Similar to Lee, Jackson preferred fighting a battle farther south at the North Anna River rather than defending Fredericksburg on the Rappahannock. According to James Longstreet, Jackson "held we would win a victory at Fredericksburg, but it would be a fruitless one to us, whereas at North Anna, when we drove the Federals back, we could give pursuit to advantage." Very little opportunity to pursue and destroy the Army of the Potomac existed after a successful Confederate defense on the Rappahannock.[127]

Lee held firm in mounting a defense at Fredericksburg in spite of his preference for the North Anna line. He would eventually fight behind the North Anna in late May 1864, but by that time he would not have the triumvirate of Longstreet, Jackson and Stuart directing his tactical operations, and he would be fighting a new Federal commander with a habit of not giving up on offensive operations.

Burnside's options were exhausted. He now sought to attack Lee's army in a manner that the Confederate commander would least expect: directly at or near Fredericksburg. Assuming that the opposition that the Federal gunboats had experienced at Port Royal indicated a significant portion of Lee's army in that vicinity, the Army of Northern Virginia had to be weak somewhere in the center of its lines. That weak center, Burnside reasoned, was Fredericksburg. Meeting with his grand division commanders at noon on December 9, Burnside laid out his plans for crossing the Rappahannock. He ordered the army engineers to lay pontoons at the upper part of the town, at the lower part of the town near the steamboat wharf and at appropriate points one to two miles south of the town, with "the grand divisions to concentrate...near the places for proposed bridges." Sumner would cross into Fredericksburg, while Franklin would operate south of town, with

Fredericksburg

Hooker acting as a general reserve to reinforce Sumner and Franklin as needed. As the grand division commanders disseminated the battle plans to their respective corps, division and brigade commanders, it became clear that Burnside's subordinate generals were not confident that they would be successful. According to Major General Darius N. Couch commanding the II Corps, "There were not two opinions among the subordinate officers as to the rashness of the undertaking."

Having heard the growing criticism, Burnside convened a meeting later that afternoon of the general officers of the army and key staff officers. Brigadier General Oliver Otis Howard, commanding a division in the II Corps, remembered a frustrated Burnside's reply to those carrying out his plans:

> *I have heard your criticisms, gentlemen and complaints. You know how reluctantly I assumed the responsibility of command. I was conscious of what I lacked; but still I have been placed here where I am and will do my best. I rely on God for wisdom and strength. Your duty is not to throw cold water, but aid me loyally with your advice and service.*

Burnside's winter campaign had serious signs of failure before things had gotten underway.[128]

Six pontoon bridges began construction at the three locations Burnside had chosen for the army's crossing in the early morning hours of December 11. Detachments of the Fiftieth New York Engineers were given the task

Federal military engineers built pontoon bridges into Fredericksburg under Confederate fire from the opposite shore on December 11, 1862. *Waud, Library of Congress.*

Confederates in Fredericksburg attempt to slow down Federal efforts of completing the pontoon bridges. *Battles and Leaders of the Civil War, vol. 3.*

of building the two bridges at the upper end of Fredericksburg (upper crossing site), with the Fifty-seventh and Sixty-sixth New York regiments from the II Corps providing infantry protection. Another detachment of the Fiftieth New York Engineers began construction of one bridge at the lower end of town (middle crossing site), with the Forty-sixth and Eighty-ninth New York regiments providing support. Detachments of the Fifteenth New York began constructing two bridges one mile below Fredericksburg at Deep Run, while the U.S. Engineer Battalion constructed the final bridge between the two being built by the Fifteenth New York (lower crossing site). The Second U.S. Sharpshooters and Tenth Pennsylvania Reserves provide infantry support for this crossing site.

The Federal engineers made initial progress as the early morning darkness and foggy mists shrouded their movements. Confederate troops did not remain idle for long as the fog lifted. Brigadier General William Barksdale's Mississippi Brigade holding the town contested the upper and middle crossings, as Brigadier General Jerome B. Robertson's Texas Brigade made attempts at the lower crossing to feel the Federal strength and slow down their passage of the river, giving time for Lee to concentrate his forces, especially Jackson's Corps strung along from Skinker's Neck to Port Royal, closer to the rest of the army at Fredericksburg. Casualties mounted among the engineers at each of the crossing sites as enemy sharpshooters blazed away under the cover of buildings or the natural terrain. The engineers had a serious time completing their tasks at the upper and middle crossing sites compared to those on the lower site. In spite of some cover fire by the protecting infantry, the engineers' operations came to a halt.[129]

Taking advantage of the high ground on the Federal side of the river known as Stafford Heights, Brigadier General Henry J. Hunt, Burnside's artillery chief, amassed 147 guns, commanding the river crossings from north of Falmouth to south of the position near Hamilton's Crossing on the other side. In addition to the army's reserve batteries, Hunt was given an artillery battery from each infantry division to augment his force. Among the responsibilities Burnside placed on Hunt was silencing Confederate artillery across the river and providing additional protection to the engineers and their supporting infantry in completing the bridges. By 9:00 a.m., Hunt's guns began the fearful bombardment of Fredericksburg in response to Confederate artillery south of town signaling the enemy river crossings.

"We could see the old town burning in many places," reported Private Henry Berkeley of the Hanover (Virginia) Artillery, a soldier who helped man a gun near Lee's headquarters on Telegraph Hill, "while old men, women, and children, and mothers with infants in their arms came in large numbers pouring out of their devoted city." Matlida Hamilton, who resided at Forest Hill near Hamilton's Crossing south of town, entered in her

Brigadier General Henry J. Hunt (1819–1889) served as chief of artillery in the Army of the Potomac and commanded the bombardment of Fredericksburg on December 11, 1862. He was one of the originators of crossing Federal troops in boats to establish protective bridgeheads protecting engineers building pontoons. *Library of Congress.*

diary that "[t]he roar of the cannons was unceasing. A cloud of smoke hung over the town." Lieutenant Tully McCrea, commanding Battery I, First U.S. Artillery, had been born in Mississippi but raised in Ohio. His guns targeted an old mill near the upper crossing to dislodge the sharpshooters. "I have since learned," he wrote, "that [the sharpshooters] belonged to my native state, the Thirteenth Mississippi."[130]

Hunt's bombardment did very little to dislodge Confederate sharpshooters. One idea, credited to Hunt but possibly originating from Major Ira Spaulding commanding the Fiftieth New York Engineers, had it to ferry infantry in boats across the river to establish protective bridgeheads, to allow for the completion of the bridges into Fredericksburg. Members of the Seventh Michigan and the Nineteenth Massachusetts of the II Corps volunteered to ferry across the river under fire to the opposite shore at the upper crossing. Likewise, volunteers from the Eighty-ninth New York of the IX Corps ferried across to secure the middle crossing at the lower end of town. Hunt's artillery on Stafford Heights renewed its cover fire on the town.

The Eighteenth Mississippi and elements of the Twenty-first Mississippi, along with a few companies of the Eighth Florida, contested the middle crossing site in Fredericksburg's lower end neighborhoods at the wharfs. Slightly to the northeast, portions of the Thirteenth and Twenty-first Mississippi helped maintain the center of Barksdale's thinly stretched line of defense on Princess Anne Street, where he had located his makeshift headquarters in the town hall. The rest of Barksdale's command consisting of the remaining companies of the Thirteenth Mississippi and Eighth Florida, as well as the entire Seventeenth Mississippi, positioned itself to slow the advance of troops ferrying across the upper crossing site.[131]

The fight for the streets of Fredericksburg was one of the few instances of urban warfare in the American Civil War where the primary units involved on both sides were regiments and companies. The town itself became an active participant and victim as boatloads of Federal soldiers traversed the Rappahannock reaching the opposite bank.[132]

Supporting Federal artillery from Stafford Heights continued to fire shells overhead, likened to a "terrible shriek" by the historian of the Nineteenth Massachusetts ("as though a woman had been hit or was bewailing the loss of husband or lover"). The Seventh Michigan, protected by the steep bank above the river from Confederate small arms fire, disembarked from their boats and surged over the bank onto Sophia Street that ran parallel to the river. Advancing toward the houses at the intersection of Hawke Street, the Michiganders could claim the capture of at least thirty Confederate prisoners. Elements of the Seventeenth Mississippi initially defending Sophia Street fell back a block to Caroline Street and held up the Seventh Michigan's advance. Within a half-hour, the Nineteenth Massachusetts had completed its passage across the river landing to the right of the Seventh Michigan's position. Additional reinforcements came in the form of the slighted Twentieth Massachusetts—"The Harvard Regiment"—consisting of several soldiers connected with one of the oldest institutions in the United States. Promised the honor of leading the advance into Fredericksburg and superseded by the Seventh Michigan and Nineteenth Massachusetts, the acting commander of the Twentieth and his men commandeered unused boats of the engineers ferrying across the river at their own discretion. Arriving on the opposite shore, this second regiment of Massachusetts men formed up behind the Michiganders and their fellow "Bay Staters" just as the first of the two bridges at the upper crossing had been completed. These three regiments were part of the Third Brigade under Colonel Norman J. Hall of Howard's II Corps division.[133]

The Seventh Michigan and the Nineteenth Massachusetts were ordered to advance up Hawke Street, with the former regiment on the left and the latter on the right, as the Seventeenth Mississippi contested every inch of ground from its position on Caroline Street. "The orders to the whole Brigade [Hall's] were to bayonet every armed man found firing from a house, this being, I believe, contrary to the rules of war, but not of course—obeyed," wrote Lieutenant Henry C. Ropes of the Twentieth Massachusetts seven days later. "In fact no prisoners were taken but the few the Michiganders took and the wounded who lay about struck by our shells." The Seventeenth Mississippi continued to hold its position, forcing the Seventh Michigan to seek cover in a blind alley off Hawke Street. The Nineteenth Massachusetts moved toward Caroline Street, crumbling the left flank of the Seventeenth Mississippi and forcing the Mississippians to fall back. Timely reinforcements from the Thirteenth Mississippi arriving from Princess Anne Street above moved to retake Caroline Street.[134]

"On reaching the main street [Caroline Street] we found that the fire came from houses in front and rear," Lieutenant John G.B. Adams of Company B, Nineteenth Massachusetts recalled. "Company B lost ten men out of thirty in less than five minutes." Forced to fall back toward the direction of the river, the Nineteenth left behind Private Michael Redding of Company D, who had been wounded and insisted that his comrades not carry him back with them in the expectation that they would soon return. Reinforcements from the rest of Howard's division rushed across the completed bridge in support of the advance.[135]

Meanwhile, the Twentieth Massachusetts received its long-awaited opportunity for glory. The "Harvard Regiment" headed along Sophia Street and situated itself between the stalled Seventh Michigan on the left and the Nineteenth Massachusetts on the right as support for a renewed effort to clear the Confederates out of Fredericksburg. Captain George N. Macy, the ranking commander in the Twentieth, led his column four abreast amid sporadic Confederate fire from nearby buildings and houses as it turned right onto Hawke Street. It was at this moment that its guide, an older Fredericksburg resident, hesitated and was killed by a Mississippi soldier's bullet. The Twentieth advanced blindly up Hawke Street and soon encountered elements of the Seventh Michigan on its left, where Macy urged them forward. The commander of the Seventh refused, pleading that he had no orders to do so. An enraged Macy reportedly replied, "Go to hell with your Regiment then" and took the lead in the advance.[136]

Soon, a murderous fire from the Thirteenth Mississippi concealed in buildings on Caroline and Hawke Streets swept the lead elements of the Twentieth Massachusetts on three sides. "Almost every ball struck," Lieutenant Ropes reported, "and a very large proportion were killed outright or desperately wounded." Captain Henry L. Abbott, with his Company I of the Twentieth, pushed through the dangerous intersection, while the captain commanding Company K swung his men to the left on Caroline Street, facing south until he was hit in the foot and shouted for Lieutenant Ropes to take command. Company A of the Twentieth Massachusetts wheeled to the right on Caroline Street facing north. The remaining companies of the regiment filled in the positions that Lieutenant Ropes's company could not fill as his numbers continued to dwindle. The Massachusetts men had control of this intersection but needed reinforcements fast.[137]

The Nineteenth Massachusetts regrouped and advanced as skirmishers through yards and houses to the right of the Twentieth toward Caroline Street to reclaim portions of the ground it had initially gained. When the men of the Nineteenth reached Caroline Street, they found the dead body of Private Redding of Company D, who had been left behind wounded. "[T] he rebels having bayoneted him in seven places," Captain Adams related. By nightfall, reinforcements forced the Thirteenth Mississippi to withdraw from its position along with the rest of Barksdale's brigade.[138]

Later, members of the Nineteenth Massachusetts on picket duty viewed the horrific aftermath of the hard-fought battle in gaining possession of the town. "The rebels lay thick among the fence, just as they had fallen, killed by round shot and shell," the regimental historian later observed. "Some

Fredericksburg

A sketch of dead Confederate pickets in the aftermath of the Federal bombardment and crossing into Fredericksburg. *Waud, Library of Congress.*

lay with their heads severed, others with arms and legs gone and still others mutilated in a terrible manner." Another historian, this time of the Twentieth Massachusetts, recalled an encounter with members of the Eighty-ninth New York that had ended with an easier time securing the middle crossing site on the south end of town from Barksdale's Mississippians. One soldier of the Eighty-ninth was found sitting by a small fire boiling a pot of coffee and feasting on a plate of roasted chicken, eating and drinking in turn "as he took the cup from his lips, coolly placed it on the dead body of a Confederate which was lying conveniently by."[139]

Sumner's grand division spent much of the following day crossing the upper and middle sites. One soldier crossing on the pontoons at the upper crossing site recalled the effects of Hunt's artillery bombardment the day before:

> *Upon reaching the opposite…bank, we saw…many dead…One dead Confederate especially attracted my attention. He was in a standing position leaning against the corner of a block-house with his gun in his hands, and all of the head above his mouth was taken off by a shell. I have read in a magazine an article describing the attitude of soldiers who maintained a lifelike attitude after death by reason of rigor mortis; but none of these equaled in peculiarity the remarkable standing position of this beheaded soldier.*[140]

Such soldier "attitudes" would be encountered in the battle to come.

Fredericksburg, now vulnerable to the occupation of Federal troops, fell victim to unrestrained looting and pilfering described in numerous diaries, memoirs and reminiscences. Lieutenant McCrea of the First U.S. Artillery, as an illustration, recalled what he had witnessed on December 12:

> *Here I saw some of the most ludicrous scenes and at the same time the most disgraceful. Our troops broke into the houses and stole everything that they could lay their hands on. Everything that they could not eat or wear they destroyed in pure wantonness. Beautiful pictures, books, jewelry, ladies dresses, silverware, and in fact all kinds of household furniture. One soldier was seen with a nice silk dress, silk bonnet, and a silk parasol. I saw another with a silver fruit stand fastened to his belt and a silver castor stand in his hand. One soldier found a lot of beehives and brought enough to feed his whole company. But there is no use in enumerating instances. Every house was completely riddled…I was surprised when we got into Fredericksburg to find so many women and children in the town who had*

A sketch of Federal soldiers taking advantage of items found in the abandoned homes and businesses of Fredericksburg. *Lumley, Library of Congress.*

been there the day before during the bombardment. Poor creatures! How I did pity them; they had not yet recovered from their fright. I talked with some of them and asked them how they felt when the cannon balls were flying so thick through the town. One poor widow woman that I asked said that she went into a cellar and prayed...How can one be surprised that they are determined never to give up. I never felt so much disgusted with this war as I did that day. I wish the war could be brought to an end and put a stop to all this terrible suffering.

Overzealous members of the Forty-eighth Pennsylvania in the IX Corps, eager to feast on "Johnny Cakes," confiscated what they thought to be flour from the storeroom of a house. When the cakes did not "brown" when cooked, the Pennsylvanians, impatient with hunger, served them, only to discover that they had appropriated plaster of Paris, prompting one of them to remark that he thought it "was Damned heavy flour in my haversack," giving new meaning to a "heavy" breakfast.[141]

The Army of the Potomac was now on its enemy's side of the river. Burnside, still formulating his plans, made an inspection tour of his lines late in the day on December 12. Intent on gaining the heights behind Fredericksburg, Burnside entrusted Sumner with this task. The II Corps under Major General Couch would have the responsibility of advancing through Fredericksburg, attacking the Confederates on Marye's Heights and occupying the position once the enemy was defeated and/or had retreated. Brigadier General Orlando B. Willcox, with the IX Corps, would act in support of Couch's operations forming on the left of the II Corps and extending south of town across Hazel Run short of Deep Run, maintaining a communications link with the units of Franklin's Left Grand Division.[142]

Afterward, Burnside inspected the positions of the Left Grand Division. The Richmond Stage (or Bowling Green) Road running roughly parallel to the Richmond, Fredericksburg and Potomac Railroad was the important thoroughfare running south of Fredericksburg and the key landmark of direction for the Federal troops poised to attack the Confederates at Prospect Hill and Hamilton's Crossing. Burnside met with Franklin and his corps commanders, Major General John F. Reynolds commanding the I Corps and Major General William F. "Baldy" Smith commanding the VI Corps, at the confiscated manor of Arthur Bernard known as Mannsfield. Burnside's subordinates pressed him to consider turning Lee's right flank with a strong attack in their sector using both corps as well as supporting units from the III Corps of Hooker's Center Grand Division. Federal engineers had faced very little Confederate opposition when building the bridges at the lower crossing site. In an unusually aggressive move uncharacteristic of his generalship, Franklin had begun crossing his command when Sumner's troops had barely organized their venture in ferrying infantry across the river to protect the bridge builders at the upper and middle crossing sites the previous day. Seeking justification for crossing the Rappahannock, Franklin requested permission to establish a strong position on the opposite bank, which was promptly denied by Burnside on the same grounds given to both Sumner and Hooker the previous month—that he did not wish to have the army separated by the river.

The generals of the Left Grand Division had agreed with their chief that Lee had fewer forces in their vicinity and were still stretched thin as far south as Port Royal. Although complete surprise might be out of the question for their operations, Federal strength in numbers could overwhelm their adversaries, preventing Lee from shifting troops from Marye's Heights since he would need those troops to repel Sumner's attacks in capturing those heights and perhaps forcing the Army of Northern Virginia to fall back farther south. After the war, Smith concluded that their plan offered to Burnside was "the only one that in our judgment offered a fair hope of success."[143]

Burnside left Franklin's headquarters with the promise of written and detailed orders later that evening presumably adopting their plan. Although Franklin and Smith in their postwar writings argued that Burnside's final orders were not what had been agreed upon at their "council of war," modern scholarship has acknowledged that Burnside intended for Franklin's command to make the primary attack (whether at Franklin's and his subordinates' suggestion or on his own), while Sumner's attacks against Marye's Heights would become a secondary operation. One contemporary indicator that Franklin's sector was intended to be the primary attack was Hooker's report after the battle. "The night previous to the attack (December 12), I was ordered to send two divisions (Sickles' and Birney's) of General Stoneman's [III] corps to the bridges…to support General Franklin," he reported. His remaining III Corps division and the entire V Corps had yet to cross the river.[144]

Although Burnside had lost the element of surprise, he had numbers on his side, as well as the uncanny ability to designate his attacks against points that held the strongest potential to fall if his subordinates executed their orders to their best ability. Robert E. Lee was cognizant of the weak points in his seven-mile defensive line that stretched from the vicinity of Taylor's

Hill across from Falmouth to Hamilton's Crossing. Two of these points were salients, or bulges, that stretched several hundred yards in front of the main lines and followed the contours of the terrain. If these salients were overwhelmed by Federals in large numbers, especially on the exposed sides, they could collapse, causing large breaches in the Confederate positions. The first salient was located at Prospect Hill just above Hamilton's Crossing in front of the Federal Left Grand Division's position, the highest elevation until Willis Hill was reached five miles to the north. The second salient, located at the base of Willis Hill and the southern end of Marye's Heights, was the Federal Right Grand Division's to capture. Lee still had troops on the march from Port Royal on the evening of December 12; should Burnside make a show of aggressive action before the Army of Northern Virginia had a complete concentration of its forces, the Confederate position would be in great jeopardy.

Burnside's detailed orders to his grand division commanders would not be completed until the early morning hours of December 13. Having left Franklin's headquarters at Mannsfield, Burnside possibly got lost in retracing his steps along his lines back to Fredericksburg. Once he arrived in town, it is possible that he sought Sumner's counsel but was unable to find him and was unaware that he had crossed the river to his headquarters at Chatham Manor (Lacy House). By the time Burnside returned to his own headquarters at the Phillips House almost two miles north of Sumner's headquarters about midnight, he had lost several hours. He more than likely spent the early morning hours preparing his orders.[145]

His first set of written orders prepared for Franklin was completed at 5:55 a.m. on December 13, 1862:

> *General Hardie will carry this dispatch to you, and remain with you during the day. The general commanding directs that you keep your command in position for a rapid movement down the old Richmond road, and you will send out at once a division at least to pass below Smithfield, to seize, if possible, the height near Captain Hamilton's, on this side of the Massaponax, taking care to keep it well supported and its line of retreat open. He has ordered another column of a division or more to be moved from General Sumner's command up the Plank road to its intersection with the Telegraph road, where they will divide, with a view to seizing the heights on both of these roads. Holding these two heights, with the heights near Captain Hamilton's will, he hopes, compel the enemy to evacuate the whole ridge between these points. He makes*

these moves by columns distant from each other, with a view of avoiding the possibility of a collision of our own forces, which might occur in a general movement during a fog. Two of General Hooker's divisions are in your rear, at the bridges, and will remain there as supports. Copies of instructions given to Generals Sumner and Hooker will be forwarded to you by an orderly very soon. You will keep your whole command in readiness to move at once, as soon as the fog lifts. The watchword, which, if possible, should be given to every company, will be "Scott."[146]

At 6:00 a.m. the same morning, written orders prepared for Sumner were issued:

The general commanding directs that you extend the left of your command to Deep Run connecting with General Franklin, extending your right as far as your judgment may dictate. He also directs that you push a column of a division or more along the Plank and Telegraph roads, with a view to seizing the heights in the rear of the town. The latter movement should be well covered by skirmishers, and supported so as to keep his line of retreat open. Copy of instructions given to General Franklin will be sent to you very soon. You will please await them at your present headquarters, where he (the general commanding) will meet you. Great care should be taken to prevent a collision of our own forces during the fog. The watchword for the day will be "Scott." The column for a movement up the Telegraph and Plank roads will be got in readiness to move, but will not move till the general commanding communicates with you.[147]

The final orders for Hooker were issued at 7:00 a.m.:

The general commanding directs that you place General Butterfield's corps and Whipple's division in position to cross, at a moment's notice, at the three upper bridges, in support of the other troops over the river, and the two remaining divisions of General Stoneman's corps in readiness to cross at the lower ford, in support of General Franklin. The general commanding will meet you at headquarters (Phillips house) very soon. Copies of instructions to General Sumner and General Franklin will be sent to you.[148]

The Battle of Fredericksburg was about to begin.

Chapter 4

A Holy and Just Cause

Prospect Hill and Hamilton's Crossing

A s dawn approached on Saturday, December 13, 1862, a group of riders emerged through the fog-draped landscape at a high eminence known locally as Telegraph Hill that served as Robert E. Lee's field headquarters. It would soon after take on the name of its occupier. Dismounting from his horse wearing a brand-new gray coat trimmed in gold lace and sporting a bluish-gray kepi-style cap surrounded by a gold band at the base and a pair of shiny new boots, the lead rider saluted Lee. Thomas J. "Stonewall" Jackson, commanding the Second Corps of the Army of Northern Virginia, had arrived for a final conference before the impending battle. The new coat had been a gift of cavalry commander J.E.B. Stuart, while the accompanying saber and spurs had been a recent gift from his wife Mary Anna. Stonewall's appearance surprised many of the officers and men who encountered him, and they almost failed to recognize him as he discarded his usual shabby and often soiled attire.

Jackson had arrived shortly after James Longstreet, commanding the First Corps, who had helped himself to the warmth of a nearby fire and was wrapped in a shawl. Stuart had also been warming himself by the fire, awaiting Jackson's arrival. When a staff officer complimented Jackson on his new uniform, he remarked, "I believe it was some of my friend, Stuart's doing."

Although the temperature at the moment was just above freezing, it would reach the sixties by midafternoon. Lee, with his headquarters at the

A postwar view of the Prospect Hill section of the Fredericksburg Battlefield on the Confederate right, looking to the northeast. The spires of Fredericksburg are barely visible on the far left. Battles and Leaders of the Civil War, *vol. 3*.

center of his lines, could ideally observe operations on both Jackson's and Longstreet's fronts. The offensive-minded Jackson proposed to Lee that he believed that the heavy fog could conceal a forceful and successful attack against the Federals; this was seconded by cavalryman Stuart. Concerned about the disparity of numbers between the two armies, Lee firmly stated that the Confederates would be best served fighting defensively to offset their lesser numbers. Lee promised to take advantage of counterattacks as opportunities presented themselves. Jackson would be sure to highlight such opportunities for his commander as the day progressed.

As part of the fog lifted on Jackson's front, revealing the mass of William B. Franklin's Federals a fourth of a mile away, Longstreet decided to have some fun at Jackson's expense. "Are you not scared by that file of Yankees you have before you down there?" he asked. Jackson curtly replied, "Wait until they come a little nearer, and they shall either scare me or I shall scare them!"

Lee requested that Jackson and Stuart accompany him on a brief inspection of Jackson's lines. As Jackson mounted his horse, Longstreet attempted another jab at his fellow corps commander: "Jackson, what are you going to do with all those people over there?" After a brief moment, Jackson responded in a more serious tone, "Sir, we will give them the bayonet!" With this sentiment, Longstreet was left behind to look after his sector of command as Lee, Jackson and Stuart rode south along the Confederate lines.[149]

Although Longstreet meant no harm in his jesting tone, J.E.B. Stuart was one of the very few people who could elicit even the least bit of humor out of Stonewall Jackson. According to one of Jackson's staff officers, Major Henry Kyd Douglas, when the army was moving south after Sharpsburg (Antietam) that fall, Stuart had arrived at Jackson's camp late in the evening after Jackson had gone to bed. Dispensing with modesty, a tired Stuart entered Jackson's tent and joined him under the blankets. Douglas recounted Jackson's reaction the next morning:

"General Stuart, I'm always glad to see you here. You might select better hours sometimes, but I'm always glad to have you. But, General" rubbing his legs *"you must not get into bed with your boots and spurs on and ride me around like a cavalry horse all night!"*

Jackson held the fun-loving Stuart in high esteem and was probably relieved that the bulk of Stuart's cavalry command was attached to the right of his position serving as a mobile defense between Hamilton's Crossing and Massaponax Creek.[150]

Lee, Jackson and Stuart passed Longstreet's divisions of George E. Pickett and John B. Hood, who made up the extreme right of his lines. Since the positions of these divisions fell farther back from the main Confederate lines in a large, concave formation, Lee expected these troops to act as a general reserve for the army. Hood, in particular, held a complex mission, since the right of his position linked with the brigades of A.P. Hill's division of Jackson's Corps. Hood would be subject to the orders of his own corps commander, Longstreet, as well as from Jackson—as circumstances dictated on his front—and, finally, from Lee.

Longstreet, prior to the high-level briefing on Telegraph Hill, had conferred with Hood, advising him of the likelihood that Jackson's front would be a major point of attack, as he could hear voices of the enemy concealed by the fog shouting the commands "Forward, guide center, march!" Longstreet ordered Hood "to co-operate with A.P. Hill or any other troops of General T.J. Jackson's corps" and urged him to attack the

Federal flank as it made contact with Jackson's lines on his right when the opportunity presented itself, giving Pickett similar discretionary orders to cooperate with Hood's movements.[151]

Given the nature of the terrain on Jackson's front, A.P. Hill's division manned the almost two-mile first line of defense from Prospect Hill near Hamilton's Crossing, running north to Hood's right flank located south of the intersection of the Lansdowne Valley Road and the military road built by the Confederates connecting their two corps. William B. Taliaferro's division formed part of the second line to the left rear of A.P. Hill. Soon, the division of Jubal A. Early would form to the right of Taliaferro, completing the second line. D.H. Hill's division, making a twenty-mile forced march from Port Royal, would form behind Taliaferro and Early, acting as Jackson's corps reserve. Jackson would have a defense in depth. Two brigades of Stuart's cavalry extended the Confederate line. Fitzhugh Lee's brigade held position between Hamilton's Crossing and the Richmond Stage Road, while W.H.F. Lee's brigade held position to the northeast on the other side of the Richmond Stage Road, near where the Massaponax began to drain into the Rappahannock.[152]

Jackson commanded veteran divisions. Two of them, D.H. Hill's and A.P. Hill's, were under their regular commanders. The division—under the nominal command of Richard S. Ewell, who had been recovering from the loss of a leg during the Second Manassas Campaign—fell to Brigadier General Jubal A. Early. Jackson's own original division he had commanded in the Shenandoah Valley earlier that spring was now commanded by Brigadier General William B. Taliaferro. Unfortunately, Jackson tended to maintain tense relationships with his subordinate division commanders, stemming from his personal eccentricities, exacting and stern orders and absolute secrecy of plans.

Graduating in the West Point class of 1842, South Carolinian Daniel Harvey Hill was the only non-Virginian commanding a division in Jackson's Corps and perhaps the only one of his subordinates who held his confidence. Yet this did not prevent his alienation within the higher echelons of the Army of Northern Virginia. Harvey Hill, a battle-hardened veteran of the Mexican-American War, possessed the stern look and erect bearing of a warrior—even if, at times, he was temporarily incapacitated by a painful childhood spinal ailment. Resigning from the U.S. Army in early 1849, Hill became professor of mathematics at Washington College (later Washington and Lee University) in Lexington, Virginia, and, still later, professor of mathematics and civil engineering at Davidson College in North Carolina.

Staunchly religious, he married Isabella Morrison, the eldest daughter of a leading Presbyterian minister in the latter state. Just before the present war, Hill was serving as superintendent of the North Carolina Military Institute in Charlotte. Hill first met Jackson in the combat zone of Mexico and took the young Virginian under his wing. In 1851, while teaching in Lexington, Hill recommended Jackson, who had recently resigned from the U.S. Army, for a teaching position at the neighboring Virginia Military Institute. Hill also credited himself with guiding Jackson in becoming a member of the Presbyterian denomination. Jackson would later marry the younger sister of Hill's wife, Mary Anna Morrison (Jackson's second marriage), making them brothers-in-law.[153]

Going with his adopted state, Hill became colonel of the First North Carolina Infantry and led this unit in one of the earliest Confederate victories in Virginia, at the Battle of Big Bethel in June 1861. He was soon after promoted brigadier general and commanded a brigade under his West Point classmate James Longstreet. By the spring of 1862, he commanded a division as a major general under Joseph E. Johnston and then Robert E. Lee. He was one of Lee's senior division commanders who thwarted McClellan's Peninsula Campaign, most notably at Gaines Mill and Malvern Hill. During the Second Manassas Campaign, Hill's division was stationed at Hanover Junction north of Richmond as a safeguard for the Confederate capital, while the rest of the Army of Northern Virginia battled Pope's Army of Virginia. This crucial assignment was a clear testament to Harvey Hill's reliability and resourcefulness as a combat commander. Hill continued his solid performance at South Mountain and Sharpsburg. It was apparent that Hill felt animosity over Jackson's rapid promotion since he viewed himself as "Stonewall's" mentor before the war, but he still revered him for his military prowess and contributions toward the Army of Northern Virginia's success.[154]

Stubborn, caustic and often condescending, Harvey Hill still cared for his men, commending them when warranted but hating "shirkers and cowards" as much as he despised Yankees. At times, he displayed an acerbic wit, as evidenced by the example given by Captain William T. Poague, commanding the Rockbridge (Virginia) Artillery, who had been a student of Hill's at Washington College before the war. "On an application from a member of a band for a furlough," Poague recalled, "he endorsed: 'Respectfully forwarded, disapproved—shooters before tooters.'"[155]

Among all the division commanders in the Army of Northern Virginia, Lee thought Ambrose Powell Hill to be the best. Lee had hoped to secure higher command responsibilities for A.P. Hill, provided he could learn to develop a thicker skin when interacting with his military equals and superiors, as well as temper his prickly sense of honor and fairness. Hill, born in Culpeper County, Virginia, had been held back a year at West Point due to illness. Graduating in 1847, Lieutenant Hill served in the artillery in the final combat actions of the Mexican-American War. Later, he served at posts in Florida and Texas before having a five-year stint with the United States Coast Survey in Washington, D.C. Hill resigned his army commission a month before Virginia passed its secession ordinance. Although believing the institution of slavery an evil, he advocated the doctrine of states' rights as the fundamental issue of the impending war.[156]

Gaining command of the Thirteenth Virginia Infantry, Colonel Hill was present at First Manassas (First Bull Run). The following spring, "Little Powell" distinguished himself in combat during the Peninsula Campaign when he was promoted to major general and placed in command of what he dubbed the "Light Division." Hill's division, the largest in the Army of Northern Virginia, would soon be recognized as one of the hardest-fighting units in the Confederacy. In the thick of battle, Hill was fond of wearing his "red battle shirt" and earned the reputation as a fighting general. His fighting reputation, while successful in battle, did not always help in his relations with military superiors. Challenging Longstreet to a duel while under his command in late June 1862, Hill was transferred along with his Light Division to Jackson's command one month later in a move that Lee hoped would cure both subordinates' shortcomings. Lee advised Jackson:

> *I will send A.P. Hill's division…to you.…Do not let your troops run down if it can possibly be avoided by attention to their wants, comforts, &c., by their respective commanders. This will require your personal attention; also consideration and preparation in your movements…A.P. Hill you will, I think, find a good officer, with whom you can consult, and by advising with your division commanders as to your movements much trouble will be saved you in arranging details, as they can act more intelligently. I wish to save you trouble from my increasing your command.*[157]

Hill soon after fought at Cedar Mountain, participated in the capture of Harpers Ferry and saved Lee's army from destruction at a crucial moment at Antietam. During the Army of Northern Virginia's advance into Maryland, Jackson placed Hill under arrest for neglect of duty. The subsequent charges and countercharges between the two generals continued

Major General A.P. Hill (1825–1865), commanding the highly reputable "Light Division" in Jackson's Corps, held the first line of defense at Prospect Hill. A dangerous gap in his line almost turned the tide of battle in favor of the Federals. *Library of Congress.*

Brigadier General Jubal A. Early (1816–1894), commanding a division in Jackson's Corps, stabilized the Confederate line at Prospect Hill, halted the Federal breakthrough and spearheaded a counterattack, halting further offensive operations by the Federal Left Grand Division. *Library of Congress.*

into the late fall, when Lee decided to put aside their bureaucratic squabble in hopes that they would reconcile. In early November, a frustrated Hill wrote to cavalry commander J.E.B. Stuart: "I suppose I am to vegetate here all winter under that crazy old Presbyterian fool." While Lee had recommended to Confederate president Jefferson Davis the appointment of Longstreet and Jackson to command his two corps, he also endorsed Hill as the next best officer in the army. "He fights his troops well," Lee observed, "and takes good care of them."[158]

Jackson's next senior division commander, Jubal Anderson Early, possessed characteristics that also tried Jackson's patience. Early, "Fighting Joe" Hooker's West Point classmate and nemesis on the slavery question, reportedly had a mess hall plate smashed over his head by fellow cadet and Virginian Lewis A. Armistead, who commanded a brigade in Pickett's division. After his graduation in 1837, Early served on active duty in Florida before resigning from the army the following year. Returning to Virginia to practice law, Early was elected to the Virginia House of Delegates and later served as a Virginia Commonwealth's attorney. A two-year interlude of service in the Mexican-American War was the only interruption of his legal practice and political career. Elected to Virginia's secession convention in 1861, Early remained an advocate for staying in the Union.[159] After Lincoln's call for volunteers to suppress the rebellion in the aftermath of the firing on Fort Sumter, South Carolina, Early joined the Confederacy. He commanded a brigade at First Manassas and continued service during the Peninsula Campaign when he was wounded at Williamsburg. Lee dubbed Early his "bad old man" for the excessive use of colorful oaths uttered in the presence of his superiors when angered. "Old Jube," was never afraid to criticize his superiors. While the Second Corps marched to Fredericksburg, Jackson penned an inquiry to Early asking "why he saw so many stragglers in the rear of your division today." Early replied to the stern disciplinarian that "the reason why the Lieutenant General commanding [Jackson] saw so many stragglers in the rear of my division today is probably because he rode in the rear of my division."[160]

William Booth Taliaferro, of both Virginia Tidewater gentry and Italian ancestry, hailed from Gloucester County, Virginia. Graduating from the College of William and Mary, he studied law at Harvard University. The Mexican-American War—not West Point like his fellow division commanders—earned him a captain's commission in the Ninth U.S. Infantry. By 1848, the twenty-six-year-old Taliaferro left the seat of war with the rank of major. He subsequently represented his home district in the Virginia House of Delegates and commanded the Virginia militia with the rank of major general following John Brown's raid on Harpers Ferry in October 1859 and his subsequent execution near Charleston, Virginia, that December. At the start of the Civil War, Taliaferro was colonel of the Twenty-third Virginia and commanded a brigade under Jackson by the end of 1862. Wounded during the Second Manassas Campaign, Taliaferro returned to duty commanding Jackson's original division that included the five Virginia regiments from the Shenandoah Valley known as the "Stonewall Brigade."[161]

Harvey Hill, Powell Hill and Early, at times, were annoying thorns in the side of their corps commander, but very few matched their abilities to lead and manage brigades in the thickest of combat. They were solid combat commanders. Taliaferro, the only one of Jackson's division commanders not to have attended West Point, also experienced Jackson's wrath at times—perhaps unfairly, since very few could attain Jackson's exacting standards when it came to those commanding his original division that he commanded with success in the Shenandoah Valley. It probably did not help Taliaferro that he was the ringleader of a petition against Jackson sent to the Confederate War Department that almost effected Jackson's resignation. One reason Jackson may have eased up on Taliaferro slightly was due to his family's prominence and political connections. Such connections, nevertheless, did not endear Taliaferro to his own soldiers, something that his fellow division commanders had had the privilege of earning in the course of the war.[162]

The retinue of Lee, Jackson and Stuart left Hood's men and soon encountered Jackson's front lines, manned exclusively by A.P. Hill. The six brigades of the Light Division were arrayed in two lines. Brigadier General James H. Lane's brigade of five North Carolina regiments held the left of Hill's first line positioned along a segment of the Richmond, Fredericksburg and Potomac Railroad. To the right of Lane, situated across the crest of Prospect Hill, was the brigade of Brigadier General James J. Archer comprising regiments from Tennessee, Georgia and Alabama. The Virginia brigade under Colonel John M. Brockenbrough formed on Archer's right on Prospect Hill, stretching to Hamilton's Crossing. Hill's second line was composed of the North Carolina brigade of Brigadier General William D. Pender, formed to the southwest of the cabins of Alfred Bernard's slaves who owned the manor known as "The Bend" near the Rappahannock about a mile and a half to the northeast. Alfred's brother, Arthur, owned Mannsfield about a mile south and that was now the headquarters for the Federal Left Grand Division. Positioned three hundred yards behind Lane's brigade and angled to the right of Pender parallel to a "military road" was the Georgia brigade of Brigadier General Edward L. Thomas. Thomas's Georgians linked to the right of Hood's brigades on the same road. The South Carolina brigade of Brigadier General Maxcy Gregg formed on Thomas's right about a quarter-mile behind the right flank of Lane's brigade and the left flank of Archer's brigade.

One glaring flaw in Hill's position was the four- to six-hundred-yard-wide gap between Lane's and Archer's brigades. Within this gap was a thick, tangled growth of trees in the midst of a swampy morass that narrowly protruded in the direction of the enemy, extending across a portion of the railroad tracks. Hill, not wishing to place his men in a cold and damp position, reasoned that if his men would have difficulty negotiating this particular terrain, so would enemy soldiers. As a precautionary measure, Hill had placed Gregg behind this gap as part of his second line, acting as a reserve to render assistance to either Lane or Archer if needed. On the previous day, J.E.B. Stuart and one of his staff officers, Prussian-born Major Heros von Borcke, had noticed this gap. "I remarked to Stuart that I thought it should be cut down," Von Borcke remembered, "He [Stuart] did not regard this as necessary, as he did not believe that, under the sweeping cross-fire of our artillery, the Federals could ever advance so far."

Jackson, a proud prewar artillery officer and VMI artillery instructor, was evidently aware of this gap. In spite of the tenuous relationship between Jackson and Hill (also a former artillery officer), both men concurred with Stuart's assessment in their estimate of how significant of a problem this gap might be in the coming battle. Lee seemed to have no major concerns with the dispositions made on Hill's line during his inspection. In this light, the disposition of the artillery on the Confederate right made a great deal of sense.

Brigadier General William N. Pendleton (Lee's artillery chief) and Colonel Stapleton Crutchfield (Jackson's corps artillery chief), along with staff engineers, devised measures to cover the gap in the center of A.P. Hill's lines. While guns could not be placed inside the gap, nor could they provide direct fire on the area without potentially hitting friendly troops, the artillery chiefs believed that the broken ground in Hill's position provided enough open fields of fire to at least obliquely defend the right and left of the gap. Accordingly, Lieutenant Colonel Reuben Lindsay Walker, Hill's divisional artillery chief, placed fourteen guns from the various batteries in the division tightly packed in the space between Archer's and Brockenbrough's Brigades on Prospect Hill. The left portion composed of eight guns of this artillery was under the command of Captain David McIntosh of the Pee Dee (South Carolina) Artillery, and the right portion of the remaining six guns was under the direct command of the bespectacled Captain William R.J. Pegram of the Purcell (Virginia) Artillery. These gunners were expected to provide indirect fire to cover the right of the gap. Prospect Hill would be the strongest position on Jackson's front.

Colonel Crutchfield borrowed the twelve-gun artillery battalion under Captain John B. Brockenbrough (no relation to infantry brigade commander Colonel John M. Brockenbrough), normally attached to Taliaferro's Division, and placed it to the left front of Lane's Brigade across the railroad tracks. It was hoped that Captain John B. Brockenbrough's gunners could lay down indirect fire covering the left of the gap. Since these guns were exposed in the open to enemy fire and might be compelled to fall back, Crutchfield placed nine guns under Captain Greenlee Davidson of the Letcher (Virginia) Artillery about three hundred yards behind the left rear of Brockenbrough's artillery by Bernard's slave cabins to continue some effort of keeping up a raking oblique fire. Finally, Stuart's artillery chief, Major John Pelham, controlled eighteen guns situated across the road from Hamilton's Crossing to the river. The guns were from Pelham's own horse artillery batteries, augmented by batteries from the general artillery reserve. In addition to guarding the right flank of the Army of Northern Virginia, Pelham's guns were in ideal positions to fire on the left flank of the Army of the Potomac.

Lee, Jackson and Stuart were joined by A.P. Hill at Prospect Hill. All were convinced that the artillery would save the day and were ready to repel any attack that Burnside's legions hurled against them. As the

Major John Pelham (1838–1863), commander of J.E.B. Stuart's Horse Artillery, began the Battle of Fredericksburg with a two-gun battery section that fired into the left flank of the Federal lines on the morning of December 13, 1862. *Library of Congress.*

Federal bombardment began against Jackson's position and a large mass of
Federal troops surged forward, Major Von Borcke, who was present, asked
Jackson if he could hold his position. "Major," Stonewall snapped back
confidently, "my men have sometimes failed *to take* a position, but *to defend* one,
never! I am glad the Yankees are coming." James I. Robertson Jr., modern-
day biographer of both Stonewall Jackson and A.P. Hill, has concluded that
both Jackson and Hill sincerely believed that they had taken the necessary
precautions in dealing with the gap in the lines. "Their mistake," Robertson
wrote, "was in not considering the possibility of a disorganized attack by a
thronging mob [of Federals] ignorant of the lay of the land."[163]

William B. Franklin, commanding the Left Grand Division of the Army
of the Potomac, must have received the shock of his career when he read
Burnside's order for the day, delivered by Brigadier General James A. Hardie,
a senior member of Burnside's staff. It was 7:30 a.m., and the generals on the
Federal left had been anxiously awaiting Burnside's orders. The meticulous
engineer, Franklin read and reread the orders, going over the meaning of the
particular phrase "you will send out at once a division at least to pass below
Smithfield, to seize, if possible, the height near Captain Hamilton's." This
did not seem to be the orders for a major attack that had been contemplated
with Burnside the previous evening. Literally taking the orders to mean
sending out a single division to "seize" rather than "carry" Prospect Hill and
omitting from his mind the portion of the phrase "at least," Franklin along
with Generals Reynolds and Smith concluded that their part in the battle
would simply be "an armed reconnaissance, or an observation in force made
of the enemy's lines."

Although Burnside's wording in his orders were faulty and in some places
vague, it was clear that Franklin was responsible for the main attack to turn
Lee's flank. Additionally, General Hardie's presence and responsibility of
sending and relaying telegraphic updates between Burnside and Franklin
reinforced the importance of the Left Grand Division's mission. Moreover,
the III Corps divisions of Birney and Sykes "at the bridges" would provide
support for Franklin's operations as reinforcements and guarding the pontoon
crossing, keeping their "line of retreat open." The fact that Burnside ordered
at least a division to take Prospect Hill highlighted the wide discretion he
gave Franklin to accomplish his mission, since he was in theory better suited
than his commanding officer to determine the size of his attacking force.
Burnside no doubt expected significant elements of both the I and VI Corps
to be part of this force. It was unlikely that Ambrose Burnside expected
anything less than a major assault by the estimated forty thousand troops of

Franklin's command augmented by an additional fifteen to twenty thousand troops from Hooker's command.

Franklin chose to follow the literal interpretation of Burnside's orders—not to undermine his chief but to protect his own reputation. Similar to Burnside at Antietam when he seemed to have earned the scorn of McClellan, Franklin had dodged becoming a scapegoat for Pope's failure at Second Bull Run and had already felt that he was a target of the politicians in Washington decidedly against his friend McClellan.[164]

The Left Grand Division commander had two corps commanders who had proven themselves brave and reliable on the battlefield so far in the war. Pennsylvanian John Fulton Reynolds leading the I Corps was considered one of the Federal army's rising stars. Graduating from West Point in 1841, Reynolds served with the Third U.S. Artillery during the Mexican-American War, during which he received two brevet promotions for gallantry. Reynolds later served as commandant of the corps of cadets at West Point when the Civil War began. Commanding a division during McClellan's Peninsula Campaign, Reynolds had gained such an esteemed reputation that the Pennsylvania governor requested and was granted his services commanding Pennsylvania militia during Lee's invasion into Maryland. Returning to the Army of the Potomac, he assumed command of the I Corps when Hooker was elevated to command Burnside's Center Grand Division at Fredericksburg. Many of the I Corps troops had served under Reynolds in Fredericksburg earlier that spring, where he served briefly as military governor

Brigadier General John Gibbon (1827–1896), commanding the Second Division, I Corps, tried to follow up on the success of Major General Meade's breakthrough on the Confederate lines. *Library of Congress.*

and provost marshal. Fredericksburg residents had been so impressed by his benevolent and evenhanded administration of their occupied town that when Reynolds was captured after the Battle of Gaines Mills, they sent a petition (that was soon after granted) to Confederate authorities asking for his release on a parole of an exchange of prisoners. Reynolds and his men were familiar with the ground that they would soon fight over but not familiar with the leadership style of William B. Franklin.[165]

Franklin had had a close working relationship with his former division commander, William Farrar "Baldy" Smith, who took command of the VI Corps when Franklin became a grand division commander. Born in Vermont, Smith graduated in the West Point class of 1845, earning his nickname due to his premature loss of hair in addition to distinguishing him from the abundance of "Smiths" serving in the army. Smith spent most of his early army career with the topographical engineers conducting surveying expeditions throughout every region of the United States and teaching mathematics at West Point. Serving as colonel of the Third Vermont Volunteers at First Bull Run (First Manassas), Smith soon gained division command during the Peninsula Campaign, serving with distinction. Identified as a staunch McClellanite, Smith's military reputation was being compromised by his tendency to criticize his superiors in a manner that created dissension in the officer ranks that trickled down to the rank and file. His perceived penchant for intrigue was only second to that of Joseph Hooker in the Army of the Potomac.[166]

Reynolds's I Corps held the extreme left of the Army of the Potomac on the morning of December 13, 1862. Its three divisions were positioned between two dwellings: Mannsfield Manor (Franklin's headquarters) and Smithfield Plantation, owned by Dr. Thomas Pratt. One division under Brigadier General John Gibbon was positioned in line of battle on the eastern edge of Bowling Green Road (Richmond Stage Road) about three-fourths of a mile from the Confederate line manned by A.P. Hill's division. Gibbon, an Old Army artillery expert and battery commander, had originally been in the class of 1846 with the likes of Stonewall Jackson but, like "Little Powell," graduated a year later as a result of illness. Born near Philadelphia, Pennsylvania, Gibbon and his family spent his formative years in North Carolina. Ironically, Gibbon and his brother, Lardner, both served as best men at the wedding of fellow transplanted North Carolinian D.H. Hill in 1848. Harvey Hill, like three of Gibbon's brothers, joined the Confederacy, while Gibbon remained in the Union. He had already tangled with Harvey Hill at South Mountain three months before, and it was possible they could meet on the field south of Fredericksburg.[167]

Mannsfield (Bernard House) Ruins had been an impressive two-story stone structure and served as Franklin's headquarters during the battle and a field hospital for wounded Federals. *Library of Congress.*

The divisions of Abner Doubleday and George G. Meade were formed right and left, respectively, behind Gibbon. Brigadier General Doubleday, having graduated in the West Point class of 1842, had been an artillery captain serving at Fort Sumter, South Carolina, when the fort was fired upon by Confederate forces on April 12, 1861. It was Doubleday, in fact, who returned the first shot. The New York native rose from brigade to division command in the Army of the Potomac by the spring of 1862 but had seen limited action at Second Bull Run and Antietam.[168]

George Gordon Meade, friend and sometimes rival of his corps commander John Reynolds, hailed from Pennsylvania. He was originally born in Spain, the son of an American diplomat. Graduating from West Point in 1835, Meade served with the Third U.S. Artillery during the Seminole Wars in Florida before resigning after a year of service to pursue a career as a civil engineer. Returning to the army as a lieutenant of topographical engineers in 1842, Meade worked on coastal surveying projects and lighthouse construction on the Atlantic seaboard and the Great Lakes before and after the Mexican-American War. He was brevetted a first lieutenant for gallantry during that war. Meade began the Civil War as a captain but was immediately promoted to brigadier general of volunteers. Possessing an irascible temper, Meade could always be found in the thick of battle in the early Virginia campaigns. Meade was the army's senior division commander and also outranked at least two present corps commanders. Actually entitled to corps command, Meade was inadvertently superseded by Brigadier General Daniel Butterfield, a non–West Point volunteer, for command of the V Corps. Desiring to put aside this slight in military courtesy, Meade assured Ambrose Burnside that he would faithfully carry out his duties in division command for the good of the service.[169]

Meade had inherited the division of Pennsylvania Reserves from Reynolds when the latter rose to corps command. The "Reserves" had been Pennsylvania units raised by Governor Andrew Curtin that had exceeded the U.S. War Department's quota for regiments. Anticipating another call for troops from Pennsylvania to be mustered into the federal service, Curtin maintained these "Reserves" for the defense of the state. These units were soon called into service but, in many instances, retained their reserve designation. Reynolds had chafed during his brief tenure commanding volunteer Pennsylvania militia during the Maryland Campaign, preferring to serve with regular troops compared to volunteers. The Pennsylvania Reserves, serving with the Army of the Potomac and that he helped train and commanded early in the war, were the only volunteer units that had earned his respect. Reynolds would make sure that Meade and

Major General John F. Reynolds (1820–1863) commanded the I Corps, Left Grand Division, Army of the Potomac. *National Archives.*

the Pennsylvania Reserves played a major role in the impending battle.[170]

About a half-mile northwest of Gibbon's Division, along the Bowling Green Road and southeast of Deep Run, was the VI Corps division of Brigadier General Albion P. Howe. Situated on Howe's left beyond the intersection of the Bowling Green Road and Lansdowne Valley Road was another VI Corps division, under Brigadier General William T.H. Brooks. Brooks's right flank was in communication support with the IX Corps division of Brigadier General William W. Burns, situated just below Fredericksburg linking both wings of the Army of the Potomac. The VI Corps division under Brigadier General John

Major General George G. Meade (1815–1872), commanding the Third Division, I Corps, achieved a breakthrough in the Confederate lines commanded by "Stonewall" Jackson. Less than seven months after Fredericksburg, Meade would command the Army of the Potomac. *Library of Congress.*

Newton formed as a reserve behind Howe's rear left and Brooks's rear right, near the Bernard plantation ("The Bend"). All three of Smith's division commanders had been West Point graduates and had proven their worth as brave leaders on the battlefield, but they were relatively new to division command. Brooks and Howe were combat veterans of the Mexican-American War, while Newton plied his engineering skills to state-side construction projects. Brooks and Howe were Northerners. Newton came from a large Virginia family based in Norfolk. His father, Thomas Newton, had served in the Virginia General Assembly, as well as almost thirty-two years in the U.S. House of Representatives. Both he and a younger brother cast their lot with the Union when the Civil War began.[171]

The cavalry brigade of five regiments assigned to the Left Grand Division under Brigadier General George Dashiell Bayard formed to the left of

Newton's division, awaiting any orders from Franklin that could range from additional reconnaissance to providing a mobile skirmish line as a prelude to assault. At twenty-six, Bayard was one of the youngest brigadier generals in the Army of the Potomac, and it was expected that he would have a major leadership role in future cavalry operations. Born in historic Seneca Falls, New York, Bayard graduated from West Point in 1856 and was assigned to the First U.S. Cavalry that had been under Colonel Edwin V. Sumner. In the summer of 1860, while serving in a detachment commanded by then lieutenant J.E.B. Stuart on the Great Plains, Bayard's left cheek was virtually destroyed by a poison-tipped arrow fired by a Kiowa Indian who had feigned surrender when he approached. It took the better part of a year and several experimental surgeries to repair and heal the damage done. In spite of his facial disfigurement, Bayard maintained a dashing and erect bearing. He was assigned as a cavalry instructor at West Point to allow for his continued recuperation while remaining on active duty. "I feel that if we have war I shall not live long," Bayard wrote to Stuart in April 1861 as secession became reality, "I have no desire to do so and shall welcome the shroud as a peaceful close." Bayard was appointed colonel of the First Pennsylvania Cavalry when the Civil War began. He performed critical service commanding cavalry in operations in the Shenandoah Valley and during the Second Bull Run Campaign.[172]

Upon his appointment as a brigadier general, Bayard expressed his future hopes to his father in May 1862:

> [A]*lthough I shall have to lead the way in every fight, I yet trust a merciful Providence will protect my life, and keep me for some greater service in defence [sic] of the Union.*
>
> *I am the youngest brigadier in the army, hurrah! My eyes are fixed on the future and new lustre [sic] for my name will be achieved, if I survive.*

Growing privately disillusioned with the progress of the war, Bayard nevertheless maintained his professionalism. His frustration may have been due in part to his impending marriage to Miss Sallie Bowman, daughter of Major Alexander H. Bowman, superintendent of West Point. "It looks as if I should not be able to leave at the time appointed for my marriage," he wrote to his father in late November, "but will have to postpone it till this campaign is over."[173]

Bayard had already attempted a reconnaissance of the area around Deep Run in front of the lower crossing site. Sending the First Pennsylvania

Cavalry north of Deep Run and the First New Jersey Cavalry to the south, Bayard's scouts moved through the dense morning fog. The Pennsylvania troopers proceeded along the Lansdowne Valley Road, where it intersected with the Richmond, Fredericksburg and Potomac Railroad, and ran into portions of Robertson's Texas Brigade of Hood's Division advancing eastward with George T. Anderson's brigade of Georgians. The First New Jersey, hearing the gunfire and catching glimpses of Confederates in pursuit of their Pennsylvania comrades, realized the difficulty in negotiating the steep banks of Deep Run amid dense foliage. The First New Jersey wisely fell back to the position held by Howe's VI Corps division, while Bayard ordered up a section of nearby artillery and the First Maine Cavalry to cover the retreat of the Pennsylvanians and halt the advance of Hood's two brigades. Hood reported killing two or three enemy troopers along with five horses. Robertson's and Anderson's brigades remained in position on the left and right of the Lansdowne Valley Road, respectively, in advance of the rest of Hood's Division. Bayard's unsuccessful efforts revealed the fact that it would be much more difficult to maintain an effective communication link between Franklin and Sumner than Burnside had hoped. Franklin's young cavalry commander hoped for another opportunity to probe the enemy's lines, as his West Point classmate, Fitz Lee, and Lee's superior, J.E.B. Stuart, were lurking about somewhere on his end of the battlefield.[174]

Franklin had given Reynolds's I Corps the responsibility to make the assault, while Smith's VI Corps kept an eye out for Reynolds's right flank while continuing to guard the lower crossing site and keeping the lines of retreat open, as directed by Burnside's orders. Birney's III Corps division received orders to cross the Rappahannock as Sickles's Division anticipated similar orders upon Reynolds's request for an additional supporting division. Reynolds chose Meade's Division of Pennsylvania Reserves to spearhead the assault, with Gibbon's Division on Meade's right providing support. Doubleday's Division would protect Meade's left, as well as the army's left flank. When Meade received his assignment, he asked Franklin if it was his intention to assault with only one division instead of an entire corps. "[T] hat is General Burnside's order," came Franklin's reply. Meade, never one to shirk dangerous responsibilities, was concerned of making useless piecemeal attacks like those at Antietam, taxing the strength of many Federal units engaged. He was also worried, for good reason, that since Antietam his own division strength had been 3,800 and only recently been elevated to about 4,500 with the addition of two "non-Reserve" Pennsylvania regiments. Thus the most senior division commander led one of the smallest divisions in the

Army of the Potomac. This was clearly a testament of not only the division's reliability under solid leadership but also the high cost that had been paid in numerous actions reducing its numbers.[175]

Present-day scholarship has criticized Franklin for entrusting the assault to the smaller of his two corps and, in turn, launching an assault with the smallest division. Reynolds's I Corps had about sixteen thousand troops on hand. Given Meade's numbers, the divisions of Gibbon and Doubleday numbered approximately four thousand and six thousand, respectively. Smith's VI Corps, on the other hand, was the largest in Burnside's army, with an estimated strength of twenty-one thousand, its three divisions averaging seven thousand each.[176]

Why not give the assignment to assault Prospect Hill and Hamilton's Crossing to Smith instead of Reynolds?

Military protocol dictated that Smith, as senior corps commander in the grand division, be given the honor to cross at the lower crossing site before Reynolds. Because of Burnside's concerns of maintaining a line of communication between the two wings of the army, Franklin logically positioned these first troops—the VI Corps—in the vicinity of Deep Run running north toward Fredericksburg to satisfy his commander's wishes. This left Reynolds to deploy to the southwest, becoming the army's left flank. Moreover, if Franklin believed that a division could accomplish the task he perceived he was given, what better troops did he have closest to the objective than Meade's veteran Pennsylvania Reserves?[177]

Meade's Division marched southward toward Smithfield, which would serve as its starting point. The Pennsylvania Reserves would have to cross a mile-wide open field that sloped into a gradual depression until reaching the Richmond, Fredericksburg and Potomac Railroad near the Confederate lines. The troops would be exposed to whatever artillery fire the enemy had arrayed against them. Reynolds planned for an artillery bombardment against the Confederates to soften their position before Meade's men advanced. Meade's division contained three brigades under Colonel William Sinclair, Colonel Albert Lewis Magilton and Brigadier General Conrad Feger Jackson. Sinclair had been an enlisted soldier serving in the artillery during the Mexican-American War. He was colonel of the Sixth Pennsylvania Reserves and had only been in brigade command for a short time. Magilton had graduated from West Point in 1846, ranking just behind Stonewall Jackson, who he would soon face as an adversary. A veteran of the Mexican-American War, Magilton had commanded the Fourth Pennsylvania Reserves since the end of 1861 and had only commanded his brigade for a month. Feger Jackson had been a devout Quaker and pacifist for much of his early life. Perhaps his exposure to war while serving as a courier for the U.S. Army in Mexico caused Jackson to raise the Ninth Pennsylvania Reserves at the start of the Civil War, to the chagrin of his fellow Quakers. Wounded at Second Bull Run, Jackson was promoted to brigadier general and brigade command. Meade had experienced veterans serving in the ranks and officers who had led at the regimental level in several battles, but his current brigade commanders combined had too little experience managing multiple regiments in battle. The assault to take Prospect Hill would prove to be their on-the-job training.[178]

Sinclair's Brigade formed the first line of attack about one hundred yards behind the Bowling Green Road. The 6th Reserves were deployed as skirmishers, while from left to right the 2nd Reserves, the novice 121st Pennsylvania and 1st Reserves held ready. The 13th Reserves ("Pennsylvania Bucktails") were detailed to support the four three-inch rifled guns of Battery B, 1st Pennsylvania Light Artillery, under Captain James H. Cooper, positioned on a knoll on Sinclair's left. As Sinclair advanced into the open plain, the remaining three batteries (twelve guns) attached to Meade's Division followed behind. Meade, realizing that Sinclair's infantry was too far ahead of the artillery, called a halt three hundred yards past the Bowling Green Road. Magilton's brigade formed behind Sinclair, with the 7th Reserves holding the left of the line, followed on the right by the 3rd, 4th and 8th Reserves. The novice 142nd Pennsylvania held the extreme right of Magilton's line. Jackson's brigade formed in column of regiments on the left flank, with the 11th Reserves in advance, followed by the 5th, 12th and 10th Reserves. The 9th Reserves were deployed as skirmishers to the left of Jackson's column. Meade's immediate objective, once he successfully reached Prospect Hill, was to gain possession of the military road accurately reported to be behind the Confederate lines, severing the link between Jackson and Longstreet. Reynolds prepared for an artillery bombardment from his position to soften the Confederate defenses before Meade and Gibbon advanced.

Gibbon's Division, slightly smaller than Meade's, formed on the right, stacking his three brigades one behind the other. He placed his most experienced brigade commander, Brigadier General Nelson Tyler, in his first line composed of five regiments. Colonel Peter Lyle's four-regiment brigade formed Gibbon's second line, and Colonel Adrian Root's five regiments made up the third. About the time Sinclair's Brigade of Meade's Division first advanced, Taylor's Brigade advanced three hundred yards beyond the Bowling Green Road, leaving one-hundred-yard intervals between the three brigades. The Thirteenth Massachusetts of Taylor's brigade surged forward as skirmishers were already encountering Confederates.

Doubleday's four-brigade division had followed Meade past Smithfield. It deployed facing south with its right flank near the Bowling Green Road. Colonel Walter Phelps Jr.'s brigade formed Doubleday's right flank, followed by the brigades of Colonel James Gavin, Colonel William F. Rogers and Brigadier General Solomon Meredith.[179]

Intermittent firing between Federal and Confederate skirmishers had been exchanged earlier in the morning from the VI Corps positions near Deep Run to the area in front of Smithfield where Doubleday protected Burnside's left flank. On Smith's front, a small ridge shielded Federal troops from direct fire from the enemy but obscured their view of Reynolds's assault to the left. Deep Run dangerously separated the VI Corps units. Federal pickets had advanced beyond the ridge. Brigadier General Francis L. Vinton, commanding one of Howe's divisions, received a bullet in his abdomen fired by Confederate pickets while inspecting his own picket line. (Vinton's Federal soldiers might have been the very ones Confederate general James Longstreet warned Hood about that same morning.) Farther south, detachments of Bayard's cavalry had been sent out beyond the railroad as skirmishers in Meade's and Doubleday's fronts encountered advancing Confederate skirmishers. "Our carbineers replied cooly and rapidly," recalled one member of the First Pennsylvania Cavalry, "holding the position for fully an hour against these odds, and until the infantry skirmishers of [Meade's] Pennsylvania Reserve corps relieved us."[180]

Confederate cavalry scouts continued to inform Stuart and his artillery chief, John Pelham, about the strength on the Federal left. Pelham, who had resigned from West Point several weeks before his graduation to join the Confederacy, was anxious to engage the enemy. His guns at Sharpsburg (Antietam) had wreaked havoc on the advancing Federal columns, and he was anxious to play a part in the coming battle below Fredericksburg. The twenty-four-year-old Alabamian would soon get his wish when he requested of Stuart permission to advance a gun toward the left flank of the Army of the Potomac. Stuart granted the request.

Pelham, with a single gun crew to man a twelve-pounder Napoleon from Captain Mathis W. Henry's Virginia horse battery, trotted down Hamilton's Crossing Road to a position where it intersected with Bowling Green Road. Situated in low ground and concealed by hedgerow growth, Pelham's gunners had clear lines of fire at the Federal left flank. At 10:00 a.m., the young artillerist gave the order to fire. The Battle of Fredericksburg had begun.

Franklin's infantry advance had ground to a halt, with men being ordered to lie down. Pelham's lone gun got off three good shots before Federal artillery from Doubleday's and Meade's positions, as well as guns just across the Rappahannock, opened up in Pelham's general vicinity to fix the exact position of the rogue gunner. Much of the responding Federal fire went over Pelham's gunners' heads. "It is glorious to see such courage in one so young," Lee reportedly remarked on Pelham from his observation on Prospect Hill. One member of Stuart's staff heard Lee make an alluding criticism of Pelham's superior, Stuart, remarking "that the young major general...opened on them [the Federals] too soon."[181]

If Stuart had allowed his artillery chief to open the battle "too soon," Pelham's lone gun had already made lasting impacts on the Federals. One of Pelham's continuing shots struck down seven members of the 121st Pennsylvania in its baptism of fire. Lieutenant John G. Simpson, commanding Battery A, 1st Pennsylvania Light Artillery, attached to Meade's Division, lost one of four guns in the initial Confederate cannonade. "So rapid and effective was their fire that I changed my front by hand, as my horses were being shot down in every direction," Simpson reported. He lost eleven men and sixteen horses when the guns on A.P. Hill's front opened up on the Federals, creating a dangerous crossfire. It was here that a private in the 121st Pennsylvania was "cut in two by a cannon ball."[182]

Doubleday's Division advanced to the left of Meade. Confederate cavalry skirmishers sent out by Fitz Lee attempted to provide some support to Pelham as he continued to fire at the Federals, change positions and fire again. Meredith's brigade of Doubleday's Division—known as the "Iron Brigade" and composed of midwestern regiments wearing distinctive black hats and having a solid combat record—surged toward Pelham's intersection. The Confederate cavalry fell back, leaving Pelham to his own devices. Soon Stuart sent a second gun to Pelham, a Blakely rifle, that was unlimbered between Hamilton's Crossing and the Bowling Green Road intersection. After firing one shot, the Blakely gun was disabled by one of two Federal batteries supporting Meredith's advance. After repeated requests from Stuart, Pelham reluctantly retired. Doubleday's entire division was now poised to remain in its present position protecting the left flank of the army and the road intersection where Pelham had been positioned, leaving Meade to advance unsupported on his left. There would now be six thousand fewer Federals in the assault.

The soldiers in the divisions of Meade and Gibbon remained prone on the ground, which was now becoming muddy as the day began to warm. Federal artillery continued to bombard the Confederate positions on Prospect Hill, with some response returned in kind, making for a tense situation for many Federals in the open plain. Meade and Reynolds rode along the ranks reassuring and encouraging the men. "A star this morning, William?" Meade asked Colonel William McCandless of the Second Reserves, pointing to his shoulder straps. When a Confederate shell killed McCandless's horse, the colonel replied, "More likely a wooden overcoat." Stonewall Jackson, not wishing to expend his ammunition in an artillery duel, ordered his batteries to cease firing to allow the Yankees to advance closer, where each shot would count. (This was the point when Jackson told Major Von Borcke that he was glad the enemy was advancing.) It would also conserve ammunition for an offensive movement when the opportunity came.[183]

By 1:00 p.m., two Federal shells scored significant hits on Prospect Hill when they destroyed the ammunition chests of Captain David McIntosh's guns to the right of Archer's Brigade. The large explosions were the unofficial signal for Meade to resume his advance.

Sinclair's Brigade, with bayonets fixed, advanced toward the dense finger of woods that concealed portions of the railroad. Feger Jackson's Brigade, which had been in column formation, swung into line, extending Sinclair's line. As Sinclair's men entered the woods and negotiated the marsh to the railroad, Jackson's men veered to the left into open ground toward a stone fence near the railroad. Magilton's Brigade followed closely behind Sinclair. Confederate infantrymen fired from elevated ground on the other side of the railroad, pinning down portions of Jackson's men. The Thirteenth Reserves, released from artillery support duty, rushed forward and plugged the gap emerging in the right of his brigade. Portions of Sinlcair's and Magilton's Brigades were meshed with portions of Jackson's Brigade as they entered the marsh, causing further command and control issues with Meade's Division. Meade himself was near the railroad cut directing the traffic of troops to their proper units, amid heavy fire, to maintain the advance.

Sinclair's men hacked their way through the marsh, losing all semblance of brigade formation. They were in the very center of the large gap in A.P. Hill's line. Magilton's Brigade was close behind the rear of Sinclair. His left began overlapping with Jackson's rear, creating more confusion and disorganization. The 142nd Pennsylvania on Magilton's right flank, without the benefit of the line of woods, came under heavy fire from Confederates north of the gap. Magilton order them not to return fire, fearing that they might mistakenly fire into Sinclair's ranks ahead. The 142nd suffered heavy casualties for following their orders that day.

By the time Sinclair's regiments crossed the railroad into the woods, Sinclair had been wounded and taken to the rear, leaving the brigade virtually leaderless. William McCandless of the Second Reserves, with whom Meade had joked earlier amid the shelling, had already entered the woods and was heading in the opposite direction from the bulk of the brigade, probably unaware that brigade command fell on him. As elements of the First and Sixth advanced up a ridge, they ran into the unsuspecting South Carolinians of Maxcy Gregg.

Several of Gregg's regiments had stacked their arms, believing that couriers from Archer on the right or Lane on the left would alert them to the Federal presence. When the Pennsylvania Reserves made their appearance through the woods, Gregg ordered his men to cease fire, thinking they were some of his own pickets falling back. The forty-eight-year-old, partially deaf South Carolina bachelor did not seem to realize that the enemy had broken his lines. By the time he did, a Federal bullet shattered his spine and mortally wounded him.

Still attempting to straighten out his lines at the railroad and returning Confederate fire from Archer's Brigade, Feger Jackson rode along his lines to steady his men and prepare for a charge. His conspicuous image, riding high on horseback through the smoke and confusion of the battlefield, made him a ready target for Archer's Tennessean marksmen. A Confederate bullet struck Jackson's mount, throwing him off. Regaining his footing on the railroad bed, Lieutenant Arthur Dehon of Meade's staff reported with orders for the bruised brigade commander. Meade's orders were never issued, as Confederate fire struck down Dehon, and Jackson received a bullet crashing through his skull. Neither Meade nor his brigadiers were able to get beyond the railroad, as much of the division had done.[184]

Portions of Sinclair's and Magilton's Brigades had shattered Gregg's South Carolina brigade and were beginning to attack the right flank of Lane's Brigade. A combination of units from all three of Meade's brigades began turning the left of Archer's Brigade, virtually collapsing it. Meade realized he had made a breakthrough but needed reinforcements to sustain his efforts. In one instance, a small number of the Second Pennsylvania Reserves forced the surrender and capture of about three hundred members of the Nineteenth Georgia in Archer's Brigade. Lieutenant Evan M. Woodward recalled this particular incident after the war:

When the men left the pit to go into our lines, from their dirty and ragged appearance, they resembled the emptying of an almshouse more than

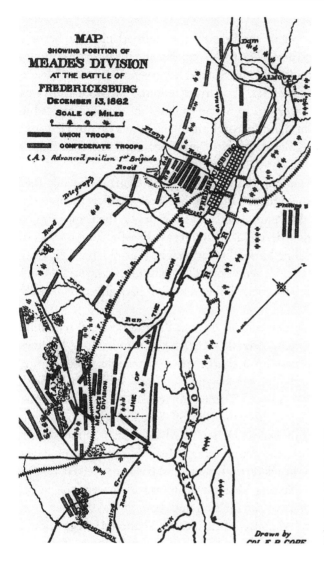

Map of the
Fredericksburg Battlefield
showing the operations
and movements of
Meade's Division on
the southern end of the
Confederate line. *Isaac
R. Pennypacker,* General
Meade.

*anything else, but under these soiled and torn jackets, there were many brave
hearts, fighting for what they believed a holy and just cause.*

Woodward had also taken the regimental flag of the Ninteenth Georgia
from its escaping standard-bearer. Not wishing to leave his command, the
lieutenant handed it to one of the men of the Second Reserves to carry it
to safety. Unfortunately, the Second Reserve soldier was struck down near
the railroad cut as he emerged from the marshy wood. A corporal of the

Above left: Brigadier General Maxcy Gregg (1814–1862), commanding a South Carolina brigade, was mortally wounded during the initial Federal breakthrough. Battles and Leaders of the Civil War, *vol. 3.*

Above right: Brigadier General Conrad F. Jackson (1813–1862), commanding a brigade of Pennsylvania Reserves, was killed in Meade's attack. Battles and Leaders of the Civil War, *vol. 3.*

Seventh Reserves took the flag to the rear, for which he would later receive the Congressional Medal of Honor. Lieutenant Woodward received the Medal of Honor three decades after the war for the flag's initial capture.[185]

Meanwhile, John Gibbon's Division had been scheduled to advance at the same time as Meade, protecting the former's right flank, as well as to broaden the front of the Federal attack, but it had been delayed due to needing additional time to arrange its brigades. By the time Meade had advanced toward the railroad cut, coming under heavy fire, Reynolds, upon Meade's urgent request, ordered Gibbon forward. The brigades of Brigadier General Nelson Taylor and Colonel Peter Lyle were arrayed one behind the other in two lines of battle. The Thirteenth Massachusetts of Lyle's Brigade led the advance as skirmishers until they ran of ammunition and withdrew as Taylor's men, slogging through the mud, reached within 150 yards of the railroad. The bulk of Lane's Confederates, positioned on the opposite side, opened fire on the advancing Federals. The Federals dropped to the ground and returned fire. The curious terrain exposed the left portion of Taylor's

Brigade, while a slight knoll in the field obscured the right portion of the brigade. By the time Taylor's left gave way, Gibbon's second brigade under Lyle arrived on the scene, coming into alignment with Taylor's remaining line, and surged forward to within 50 yards of Lane's position. Met with heavy small arms fire, the Federals fell back to the knoll. Running low on ammunition, Lyle requested Gibbon for reinforcements. Gibbon's last brigade, under Colonel Adrian R. Root, formed up for the advance. Placing three of his regiments in a line of battle with his remaining two stacked behind on the right (resembling an upside-down "L"), Root ordered his men to fix bayonets. As Root's men passed through Taylor's and Lyle's men, Lyle began withdrawing his units to replenish their ammunition. A shocked Root expected these troops to support his charge; it would prove to be a piecemeal attack, sapping away any strength and potential success Gibbon's assault

might have had. Successfully rallying units of the other two brigades, Root advanced across the railroad, hitting Lane's Confederates and swiftly locking both sides into close quarters combat. Unable to hold his position from a frontal assault as well as fire on his right flank from some of Meade's troops, Lane fell back from the railroad. Both Meade and Gibbon had successfully exploited the gap in A.P. Hill's line, but reinforcements were sorely needed.[186]

Gibbon, by happenstance, encountered George Stoneman, commanding the III Corps, whose two divisions were on loan to Franklin's Left Grand Division. One division under Brigadier General David B. Birney had been placed under Reynolds's control, making Stoneman

Brigadier General George Stoneman commanded the III Corps, Center Grand Division, Army of the Potomac. Two of his divisions were sent in support of Franklin's operations against Prospect Hill, and a portion of a third division participated in an assault against Mayre's Heights. *Library of Congress.*

a general without a command. Nevertheless, Stoneman detached three regiments from Birney's Division to provide support for Gibbon's artillery battery. Reynolds had ordered Birney's Division to take cover behind Meade's position on the Richmond Stage Road. In addition to having three regiments detached by his nominal corps commander, Birney had lost contact with one of his three brigades due to a mix-up in communications and was still subject to the orders of an additional corps commander and grand division commander not in his normal chain of command. Soon after, Meade sent back staff officers for reinforcements that would presumably come from Birney's Division. The response from Birney on Meade's first two requests for reinforcements was that he was under orders to Reynolds and not his subordinates. An angry Meade personally sought out Birney on the field. After giving Birney a biting tirade, Meade personally assumed all authority and responsibility for Birney's reinforcements by his superior rank as major general. The fight for Prospect Hill hung in the balance, with the tide shifting to either side.[187]

Jubal Early's four-brigade division waited in the woods behind the right rear of A.P. Hill's front-line position. Early thought that the infantry firing in front had gotten "quite animated" when a courier from Archer's Brigade arrived pleading for reinforcements and assistance in rallying his shattered brigade. At about the same time, Early received orders from Stonewall Jackson to have his division in readiness to make a move to the right of the railroad behind D.H. Hill's Division. As Abner Doubleday's Federal division had shifted farther south on the Richmond Stage Road, Jackson believed that the Yankees were planning a major movement in that quarter and wanted to respond in kind, shoring up J.E.B. Stuart's position with additional infantry. The situation "caused me to hesitate a moment about sending a brigade forward," Early later reported. The moment passed, with Early choosing to send Colonel Edmund N. Atkinson's Georgia Brigade to plug the breach in Hill's lines that had gotten much wider with the influx of Federals while he prepared the rest of his division to move as Jackson had ordered. The arrival of Lieutenant Ham Chamberlayne, adjutant of Reuben L. Walker's artillery battalion, only confirmed the collapse of Archer's position and the seriousness of the Federal breakthrough. Early decided to send his former brigade under Colonel James A. Walker to the front and was followed by Colonel Robert F. Hoke's North Carolina Brigade. His remaining brigade of Louisianans under Brigadier General Harry Hays took position along the railroad below Prospect Hill, where Colonel John M. Brockenbrough's Brigade had been but had fallen back when Archer's Brigade had collapsed. The feisty Early would deal with

Hays's Louisiana
Brigade of Early's
Division prepares for
action near Hamilton's
Crossing. *Battles and
Leaders of the Civil
War, vol. 3.*

the repercussions for disobeying Stonewall's orders at a later time. Lieutenant Chamberlayne would help guide some of Early's men over the unfamiliar ground to stem the flood of Federals, to protect the artillery on Prospect Hill and relieve Fredericksburg and the surrounding area of the Yankee menace.[188]

Atkinson's men maneuvered through the difficult terrain and quickly flushed out portions of Meade's Pennsylvanians, reestablishing Archer's original position. Walker moved to the northeast, running into portions of Taliaferro's Division until his brigade reached the north end of Archer's original position and engaged the pockets of Federals in the area. Lieutenant Samuel Buck of the Thirteenth Virginia in Walker's Brigade remembered driving the Federals from the railroad tracks. During a temporary halt, Buck noticed a soldier sitting quietly. "With a view of ordering him to work," the Confederate officer recounted, "I turned to him and to my surprise he was dead, having been shot in the head while looking over the railroad track." The soldier's gun was still clasped in his hands.

As Lane fell back to reform his brigade, Pender's North Carolinians rendered necessary assistance in bolstering his position while continuing to support Davidson's artillery group near Bernard's cabins. Meade's breakthrough was over as his troops became locked in bitter combat with Confederate reinforcements trying to hold on to the ground they had hoped to exploit. Many ended up falling back through the wooded area and across the railroad tracks. Confederate pursuit was only minimal due to their exposure to Federal artillery fire.

Upon Meade's third, strongly worded verbal request, Birney attempted to assemble his scattered division to reinforce Meade. Brigadier General J.H. Hobart Ward's Brigade was the nearest unit Birney had on hand. Perceiving the deterioration of Meade's right line, Ward immediately sent two New York regiments under the division commander's older brother, Colonel William Birney, to the contested railroad. Ward followed behind, personally leading the Fourth Maine. As the northernmost New York unit entered the wood, it was met by a stampede of Pennsylvania Reserves heading to the rear, overwhelmed by the release of Confederate reinforcements. Ward's men sought cover in ditches along the railroad embankment, exchanging fire with Atkinson's Georgians.

Encouraged by their success, Atkinson led a charge to the edge of the swampy woodland, preventing it from being breached again. Hoke's, Archer's and portions of John M. Brockenbrough's Brigade to the north heard Atkitson's charge and surged forward in support, hitting the left of Meade's tenuous lines holding the stone wall beyond the railroad tracks. This portion of the Confederate line halted its advance as the troops saw portions of Doubleday's Division shifting into position and began to feel the impact of the continuous shelling of Federal artillery. Atkinson continued his charge unsupported as Ward's men fell back. The Federals were now worried about the capture of exposed artillery. One of Birney's brigades under Brigadier General Hiram G. Berry was positioned to the left of the vulnerable artillery battery, while the three previously detached regiments under Colonel Regis de Trobriand were positioned to the right, creating a dangerous gap in Birney's command. Ward's Brigade had originally filled the gap for which Atkinson seemed to be heading. Drawn to the unsupported Second Maine Battery under Captain James A. Hall, and attempting to limber up and fall back to safety, Atkinson's men were able to surround an abandoned piece the battery had to leave behind in their haste. At that moment, four Federal batteries opened fire on the Confederate lines to cover the Federal retreat. One Federal battery specifically targeting Atkinson's column slowed its momentum, while De Trobriand's three-regiment command kept the Georgians in check.

Birney's missing brigade under Brigadier General John C. Robinson arrived on the scene. Birney and Robinson led the six regiments forward to protect the Federal artillery and at least regain some lost ground pushing the Georgians back to their original lines. Robinson's men surged past their artillery and exchanged fire with the Georgians as close as thirty yards in between, with heavy casualties for both sides giving the general area the name "Slaughter Pen." Unable to maintain continuous small arms fire against fresh troops, Atkinson's men under Colonel Clement A. Evans fell back to the main Confederate lines (Atkinson had been separated from his command and was later captured by the Federals).[189]

Gibbon's attempt to resume his advance had stalled about the time Atkinson's men charged the exposed Federal artillery. A.P. Hill was able to dispatch his remaining reserve brigade under Colonel Edward L. Thomas to regain his line to the north after a stubborn fight. Thomas was reinforced by Lane's reformed brigade and Pender's North Carolina Brigade, now under Colonel Alfred Scales (as a result of William Pender's wounding). Colonel Root expressed his concerns to Gibbon about the increase in Confederate reinforcements making an advance difficult. Reassuring his brigade commander that their own reinforcements were forthcoming, Gibbon rode to the right of his lines along the railroad. A shell fragment slashed Gibbon's wrist and hand, forcing the division commander to relinquish command to Brigadier General Taylor. As he headed to the field hospital for treatment, John Gibbon saw several units sitting idle. No further reinforcements beyond those of Gibbon's Division that had fallen back to resupply their ammunition would be coming. The three Confederate brigades of Thomas, Lane and Scales launched an attack against Gibbon's Division under Taylor to recapture the railroad. First, the Federal left flank crumbled to the advancing Confederates charging down the railroad ditch. Then the Confederates charged head-on into Taylor's position, causing him to issue orders to evacuate their hard-fought gains. The Confederates, too, fell back to their original positions behind the railroad, seeking safety from the horrific Federal shelling. Left behind in a virtual no man's land were pockets of Federal and Confederate soldiers, huddled down in ditches and depressions in the ground and trapped between the lines awaiting the final victor on the field. After four and a half hours of battle, the fight for Prospect Hill was over.

Meade, in a rage and on his way to Smithfield Manor to reform his division, encountered Reynolds. "My God General Reynolds, did they think my division could whip Lee's entire army?" If Meade had not gained a victory for the Army of the Potomac with his short-lived breakthrough at Prospect Hill, he had most certainly left no room for doubt that he was more than qualified for corps command.

Both sides spent the subsiding battle strengthening their lines. At Franklin's headquarters at Mannsfield, a group of officers gathered in the front yard, chatting before retiring for a late lunch. Among them was Franklin's cavalry commander, George Bayard, who Franklin had asked to remain near him in case his troopers were needed. Confederate artillery, probably surmising the location of Franklin's headquarters, began shelling the house and yard. While other officers sought cover, Bayard calmly continued his conversation with Captain H. Gates Gibson while sitting at the foot of a tree. As Bayard stood up, a shell screamed overhead, striking the ground and ricocheting into Bayard. While Gibson only suffered from having his sword belt torn off, along with a piece of his overcoat, Bayard's thigh was shattered to the hip bone. "I looked round & saw him seated in the same position," Franklin wrote to his wife. "He had that unmistakable expression." Clearly going into shock, Bayard was taken into the house, where the surgeons pronounced his wound to be mortal. Dictating final messages to family and loved ones, as well as arranging his personal effects, the promising young cavalry commander died the next day. His body was laid to rest in Princeton, New Jersey, six days after his mortal wounding and the very day he was to be married.[190]

Brigadier General George D. Bayard (1835–1862) commanded a cavalry brigade attached to Franklin's Left Grand Division. A Confederate shell permanently ended any hopes for this promising young officer to ever exercise higher command. *Battles and Leaders of the Civil War, vol. 3.*

The repulses of Meade and Gibbon, in addition to Bayard's wounding, placed Franklin in a defensive-minded mood. When Burnside sent a staff officer to ascertain Franklin's situation and to renew his assaults, Franklin noted that he believed that he would need his entire grand division in addition to the III Corps divisions just to maintain his present position. Two brigades from William W. Burns's IX Corps division had taken up position guarding the lower crossing site, while Newtown's VI Corps division shifted south near Smithfield to cover the Richmond Stage Road.

Federal and Confederate pickets at Deep Run north of Franklin's position had skirmished throughout the day, while the major fighting raged farther south at Prospect Hill and, later, farther north at Marye's Heights. After Gibbon's Division fell back, Pender sent the Sixteenth North Carolina to occupy the area when it encountered a volley from the Fifteenth New Jersey, which was hidden in the woods. Forcing the North Carolinians back toward the railroad, "Baldy" Smith ordered Brooks's Division to reinforce his picket lines covering

Deep Run. Portions of Brigadier General Alfred T.A. Torbert's New Jersey brigade, augmented by two additional regiments from Brooks's Division, were picked for the mission. The Sixteenth North Carolina retreated beyond the railroad embankment and past Davidson's artillery group, which soon opened up on the pursuing Federals. One of Davidson's battery commanders, believing that the entire Confederate picket line had collapsed, appealed for assistance to the nearby infantry brigade of Brigadier General Evander M. Law of Hood's Division. Hood had already sanctioned Law to use his discretion in assisting Pender as needed. Law swung his composite brigade of Alabamians and North Carolinians into action. The combination of Law's infantry fire, Davidson's artillery and fire on the right flank of Torbert's men from the Eighth Georgia of George T. Anderson's Brigade forced the Federals to call for reinforcements. As those reinforcements arrived, they soon found themselves under heavy shelling by Confederate artillery, compelling Smith to order Torbert's withdrawal before a general engagement developed. This was not what Smith or Franklin had in mind.

As the Federals gave up the railroad, Law pressed forward toward the Richmond Stage Road, inadvertently reaching a gap between Birney's III Corps division and Howe's VI Corps division. Fortune shined on the Federals as Sickles's III Corps division, summoned by Franklin to leave its position near the lower crossing site, was marching toward Mannsfield when ordered to wheel around to plug the gap in the nick of time as the New Jersey soldiers retreated past them. Law's Brigade now encountered a force larger than had been anticipated: Sickles's Division and a portion of Howe's. Law's men fell back toward the railroad.

It was at this time that George Pickett, itching to get into the fight, urged Hood to launch a much larger counterattack against the Federals, as Longstreet had earlier recommended at their discretion. But Hood declined to pursue anything further beyond authorizing Law to go into action. "My men were eager to be in the midst of the fight," Pickett wrote to his wife, "and if Hood had not been so cautious they would probably have immortalized themselves." Given Hood's responsibility to be subject to the orders of Longstreet, Jackson and Lee, as well as serving as part of the army's general reserve, it is possible that he did not want to stretch his forces too thin.[191]

Casualty figures for both sides at Prospect Hill were more equalized, with Jackson's Second Corps totaling 3,398 while Franklin's Left Grand Division and other attached Federal units tallied 5,333. The fighting in this sector was clearly a pitched battle—whoever emerged victorious here would become victorious in the overall battle.[192]

Chapter 5

They Were Too Proud to Retreat

The Slaughter of Fredericksburg

E dwin Sumner, commanding Burnside's Right Grand Division, probably did not relish the mission when he received his orders. Although preferring to have crossed the river, capturing Fredericksburg and the heights behind it, as soon as he arrived, Sumner understood his commander's concern. "I had had [a] little too much experience on the peninsula [McClellan's Peninsula Campaign] of the consequence of getting astride of a river to risk it here," he later reasoned. Nevertheless, the old dragoon warrior believed that had the pontoon bridges arrived when his troops had, Federal forces would be in possession of Fredericksburg and much closer to Richmond before major operations ceased for the winter. Sumner had been ordered to remain at his headquarters at the Lacy House rather than accompany his command into Fredericksburg, "owing to a special understanding...related to his supposed rashness," according to one of his subordinate generals.[193]

Similar to Franklin, Sumner followed his orders to the letter, assigning a division "supported closely by a second." But the difference was the fact that Sumner and his subordinates understood their part in the battle as being part of a secondary attack in support of Franklin's main attack. The main force assaulting Marye's Heights would be Sumner's former command, the II Corps, now under Major General Darius Nash Couch. Couch, a West Point classmate of Stonewall Jackson's, had served in the artillery during the Mexican-American War. He took a leave of absence in 1853 from the army to accompany a scientific expedition team to northern Mexico. Resigning

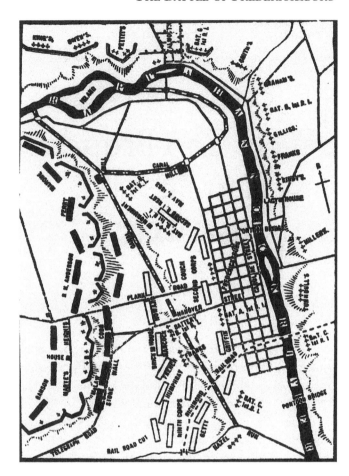

Map of the Fredericksburg Battlefield showing the operations of Battery B on the northern end of the Confederate line. *John E. Rhodes, History of Battery B: First Regiment Rhode Island Light Artillery.*

from the army in 1855, Couch ran businesses in New York City and in his native Massachusetts. By March 1862, Couch had risen from commanding a Massachusetts infantry regiment to division command. He was now one of the senior ranking corps commanders in the Army of the Potomac.[194]

Sumner ordered the IX Corps under Brigadier General Orlando Bolivar Willcox to operate on Couch's left and extend his three divisions to the south to connect with Franklin's Left Grand Division. The IX Corps, Burnside's old command, had only been attached to the Army of the Potomac since the end of Pope's Second Bull Run Campaign. Willcox, a Michigan native, practicing attorney and veteran of the Mexican-American War, had been a West Point classmate of Burnside's. He had led a brigade at First Bull Run, where he was captured after leading repeated charges against enemy forces (he was later awarded a Medal of Honor for these actions). Upon

Major General Darius
N. Couch (1822–1897)
commanded the II Corps,
Right Grand Division, Army
of the Potomac. All three of his
divisions made assaults against
the stone wall at Marye's
Heights. *Library of Congress.*

Brigadier General Orlando
B. Willcox (1823–1907)
commanded the IX Corps,
Right Grand Division,
Army of the Potomac. The
IX Corps was Burnside's
command before his
elevation to army command.
National Archives.

his release on exchange, Willcox commanded a division in the IX Corps at South Mountain and Antietam.[195]

Couch had three divisions under his command. Since units of O.O. Howard's Division had braved the fire of William Barksdale's Mississippians in protecting army engineers completing the pontoons and eventually taking possession of Fredericksburg two days before, Couch chose Brigadier General William Henry French's Division to make the attack, supported by the division of Brigadier General Winfield Scott Hancock. French, a West Point classmate of Joseph Hooker and Jubal Early, hailed from Baltimore, Maryland, and was an artillery veteran of the Seminole Wars and the Mexican-American War. A brigade and division commander in the Army of the Potomac during its earliest inception, French was called "Old Blinky" by his men for an incessant squinting of his eyes. His main claim to fame was having been Stonewall Jackson's commanding officer in Florida in the early 1850s. Their constant charges and countercharges against each other (reminiscent of Jackson's and A.P. Hill's current feuding) caused Jackson in part to resign from the prewar army.

Winfield Scott Hancock graduated from West Point in the class of 1844. A career infantry officer on the frontier and veteran of the Mexican-American War, Hancock was promoted to brigadier general in late 1861 and led a brigade under William "Baldy" Smith in the opening battles of McClellan's Peninsula Campaign, earning him the sobriquet "the Superb." His high reputation among his own men and his fellow officers came from his sheer physical bravery on the battlefield, with a touch of admirable arrogance and audacity. He attained division command before Antietam.

Oliver Otis Howard, commanding Couch's remaining division, would protect the upper portions of Fredericksburg and the army's extreme right flank as the attack commenced. Howard, a Maine native and 1855 West Point graduate, was one of the youngest division commanders in the Army of the Potomac. Committed to antislavery principles and devoutly religious during his tenure as a cadet, Howard had been ostracized by many of his fellow cadets from the Southern slave states. Ironically, it was his classmate J.E.B. Stuart of Virginia who befriended the beleaguered Howard and helped mitigate any negative feelings toward him. What drew together these two cadets possessing opposing views of the sectional tensions was their shared interest and attendance of Bible classes and prayer meetings led by West Point's chaplain and professor of ethics. Howard had served as an ordnance officer and a West Point mathematics instructor, as well as was a veteran of the later Seminole Wars in Florida. Commanding a brigade during the

Above: Brigadier General William H. French (1815–1881), commanding the Third Division, II Corps, led the first major assault against Marye's Heights. *Library of Congress.*

Right: Brigadier General Winfield Scott Hancock (1824–1886), commanding the First Division, II Corps, led the second major assault against Marye's Heights. Among his assaulting troops were the five regiments that made up the famous Irish Brigade. *Library of Congress.*

Brigadier General Oliver O. Howard (1830–1909), commanding the Second Division, II Corps, led the third major assault against Marye's Heights. *Library of Congress.*

Peninsula Campaign, Howard lost his right arm in the Battle of Fair Oaks (Seven Pines). Often called the "Praying General," Howard's personal bravery on the battlefield was never in doubt.

Howard held command at Fredericksburg since its initial occupation on December 11 as the rest of Sumner's Right Grand Division crossed over the pontoons. On the morning of December 13, as Howard and his staff breakfasted and held an impromptu prayer meeting appealing to a higher power for Federal success, an older resident of Fredericksburg was present. Shaking her head after Howard finished the morning prayers, the old woman said to the Yankee general from Maine, "You will have a Stone wall to encounter, Hills to climb, and a Long street to tread before you can succeed." This ominous warning was not too far from the truth if applied to the Army of the Potomac. Federal troops would have to encounter the Confederates of Stonewall Jackson, A.P. Hill, D.H. Hill and James Longstreet. More specifically, Howard's division and the other divisions making up the Right Grand Division would definitely encounter the Confederate First Corps of James Longstreet—and the Federals would indeed have a memorable tread in attempting to reach the enemy position.[196]

The path before the II Corps—running from the western edge of Fredericksburg to the foot of Marye's Heights—was about one mile of open plain dominated by the town fairgrounds and a sprinkling of homesteads and subsidiary buildings. Running diagonally from southeast to northwest midway on the plain was a canal ditch, or millrace, that provided a spillway for the Rappahannock canal to the north. The ditch, fifteen feet wide and five feet deep, was flanked on both sides by stone and wooden boards.

A view from the Federal perspective. The road to the right is possibly Hanover Street leading west out of Fredericksburg. Marye's Heights is to the left center in the background. The columns of Brompton (Marye House) are barely visible through the trees on the heights. *National Archives.*

Unfortunately, three feet of water remained in the ditch. It would remain one of the major obstacles in the Federals' path of attack. Frederick Street to the south and Hanover Street to the north would mark the general flank boundaries of the initial Federal attacks.

Another major obstacle were the Confederate artillery batteries arrayed on the crests of Marye's Heights and the smaller Willis Hill to the south. Colonel James B. Walton held several command responsibilities in the First Corps of the Army of Northern Virginia. He served as Longstreet's de facto corps artillery chief, he commanded the two artillery battalions that made up the corps artillery reserve and he was the nominal commander of the Washington Artillery Battalion of New Orleans, which had a history dating back to 1839. Three of his four-gun batteries were arrayed facing east in freshly dug gun pits. Captain Benjamin F. Eshelman's battery held the southern end of the terraced Willis Hill with two twelve-pounder Napoleon guns in one pit and two twelve-pounder howitzers in a second pit. Captain Merritt B. Miller's battery was unlimbered to the left of Eshelman with two twelve-pounder Napoleon guns in a pit. Captain Charles W. Squires commanded a section of his battery consisting of a

A view of the plain west of Fredericksburg from the perspective of the assaulting Federal divisions. Marye's Heights, the Federal objective, is the large hill in the background of the photograph. The canal ditch (or millrace) that made Federal movements difficult under fire can be seen in the foreground. *National Archives.*

A view of Fredericksburg from the Confederate perspective. Confederate artillery occupied these positions on Marye's Heights. *Library of Congress.*

three-inch rifle and ten-pounder Parrott gun on the northern edge of Willis Hill, directly in front of the Willis Hill Cemetery. This particular artillery section was positioned south of Brompton, the Marye family home, from which the heights received its name. Squires moved another section of his battery consisting of a lone ten-pounder Parrott gun under Lieutenant John M. Galbraith north of Hanover Street in line with Brompton. North of Galbraith's position on the other side of the continuation of William Street leaving Fredericksburg, where it became part of the Orange Plank Road, was the four-gun Donaldson (Louisiana) Battery under Captain Victor Maurin attached to Anderson's Division.

Lieutenant Colonel Edward Porter Alexander, a prewar army engineer commanding the second battalion of the First Corps artillery reserve, had assisted Lee's staff engineers in locating and placing the very artillery positions that the Washington Artillery occupied. When the army commander protested Alexander's placements on Marye's Heights, preferring the gun emplacements to be moved farther back, Alexander explained that the artillerists would have the advantage of a commanding view of anything coming from their side of the river. "[B]ut [Lee] rather sat on me & had the last word, though I knew I was right & did not give it up," the young artillerist recalled. Alexander, believing that Burnside would actually attack the weaker left flank of the Confederates held by Richard Anderson's Division, placed his artillery batteries in reserve beyond the Orange Plank Road and above their lines in positions that could form "a nucleus of a second line in case [we] were compelled to fall back or change fronts."[197]

The exact center of the Federal attack would land where the left flank of McLaws's Division overlapped with the right flank of Ransom's Division, positioned in front of Marye's Heights, creating a third obstacle for the attacking Federals. Ransom's two brigades of North Carolina infantry occupied reserve positions behind the crests of Marye's Heights and Willis Hill,

Brigadier General Robert Ransom Jr. (1828–1892), a division commander in Longstreet's Corps, provided reinforcements for McLaws's troops on Marye's Heights and behind the stone wall. Battles and Leaders of the Civil War, *vol. 3.*

Above: Brompton (Marye House) was the home of the Mayre family and from which the heights derived its name. It served as McLaws's headquarters during the battle. *Library of Congress.*

Left: Major General Lafayette McLaws (1821–1897), a division commander in Longstreet's Corps, commanded Confederates on Marye's Heights, Willis Hill and Telegraph (Lee's) Hill to the south. His troops manned positions behind the stone wall in front of the Sunken Road. *Library of Congress.*

providing infantry support to the Washington Artillery. The natural terrain of Marye's Heights created a natural salient stretching forward of the main lines and that could potentially collapse in the wake of a successful Federal assault. The Twenty-fourth North Carolina Infantry of Ransom's Division occupied positions behind the Telegraph Road that ran north to south in the area between Hanover and William Streets. As the Telegraph Road continued south, hugging the base of Marye's Heights, it became flanked on both sides by stone retaining walls. It was here that the road, after years of heavy travel, took on a sunken appearance, which Confederate infantrymen used to their advantage by turning the road and wall into a long, protective rifle pit. In this particular section of the Telegraph or Sunken Road, to the right of the Twenty-fourth North Carolina, three Georgia units of Brigadier General Thomas R.R. Cobb's Brigade of McLaws's Division would hold their ground. Cobb also placed the Sixteenth Georgia Infantry near a mill behind Willis Hill in reserve. When Richard Anderson expressed his concern to Longstreet that he might not be able to hold his position should Burnside choose to attack the left flank (as Alexander had also expected), the First Corps commander sent a dispatch to Cobb asking him to conform his movements with Anderson should he have to fall back. Cobb reportedly replied after reading Longstreet's note, "If they wait for me to fall back they will wait a long time."[198]

Alexander believed that Anderson and Cobb had very little to worry about and said as much to Longstreet. "General, we cover that ground now so well that we will comb it as with a fine-tooth comb," he boasted to the First Corps commander on his placement of the artillery. "A chicken could not live on that field when we open on it." Alexander believed that Marye's Heights would be the last place Burnside would consider attacking. Longstreet and his divisions were ready to repel anything and everything the Federals threw against them.[199]

Lafayette McLaws, Longstreet's senior division commander, hailed from Augusta, Georgia, and received his given name because of his father's worship of George Washington's revolutionary ally, the Marquis de Lafayette. Graduating from West Point in 1842, McLaws spent his early army career as an infantry officer serving in post in the Indian Territory (present-day Oklahoma), Louisiana and Florida. Initially sidelined from combat action in the Mexican-American War as a result of being shot accidently by a fellow officer, Lieutenant McLaws did participate in the Battle of Monterrey and, later, the Siege of Veracruz. He commanded several companies as a senior captain in the Utah expedition against the Mormons in 1858 and 1859, as well as led an expedition in New Mexico against the Navajo people prior to his resignation in 1861. Joining the Confederacy as a colonel commanding the Tenth Georgia Infantry, McLaws rose to division command by May 1862, making him one of Lee's veteran commanders on the battlefield. Solid and dependable when fighting from a defensive position under the careful direction of his military superiors, he often lacked aggressive initiative when opportunities presented themselves. In spite of a reputation for slowness (also attributed to his corps commander, Longstreet), he was held in high esteem by his men in caring for their welfare and attending to the details of his division.[200]

McLaws's fellow First Corps division commander, Richard Heron Anderson, had graduated in the same West Point class. A South Carolina native, Anderson served in the U.S. Dragoons during the Mexican-American War. He spent the postwar years at the Cavalry School of Practice at Carlisle Barracks, Pennsylvania, and at various military posts in Texas. He spent 1856 and 1857 quelling the violent disturbances in "Bleeding Kansas" and conducting army recruits for duty in the Utah Territory in 1858. The South Carolina legislature, in a joint resolution, presented its beloved son with a sword for his service in the Mexican-American War. The key to Anderson's character was his modesty, which affected how others would view him in his future military career in the Confederacy. Resigning his commission in 1861, Anderson commanded Confederate forces in Charleston, South Carolina, and in Florida before commanding a brigade during the Peninsula Campaign. Attaining command of a division in the summer of 1862, Anderson fought in all of the major campaigns and battles of the Army of Northern Virginia for much of the year. Wounded at Antietam, Anderson proved an intelligent, solid and capable combat commander who seemed to his contemporaries unable or unwilling to exercise the full extent of his natural martial abilities.[201]

John Bell Hood, a Kentuckian by birth, claimed Texas as his adopted state when he offered his services to the Confederacy. Graduating from West Point in 1853, Hood was already a veteran cavalry officer on the western plains, having received a severe wound, in one instance, during hand-to-hand combat with hostile Indians. This personal tenacity in close quarters combat translated to the combat performance of his own Texas Brigade that he commanded during the Peninsula Campaign. His aggressiveness and personal leadership on the battlefield placed him only second to the likes of A.P. Hill. By the fall of 1862, Hood was in division command and often given the crucial assignment of being at the center of the Army of Northern Virginia, linking the commands of Longstreet and Jackson in battle.[202]

They Were Too Proud to Retreat

Although Longstreet and most of his division commanders represented the non-Virginian contingent in the army's upper leadership, George Pickett ironically was the lone Virginian in division command and, arguably, Longstreet's favorite among his other division commanders. Graduating at the bottom of the West Point class of 1846, Lieutenant Pickett had served with the Eighth U.S. Infantry with then lieutenant James Longstreet at the successful storming of Chapultepec Heights in 1847. Pickett had recovered the regimental flag when it fell from Longstreet's hands upon his wounding and sustained the initial breakthrough against the Mexican bastion that was key to the capture of Mexico City. Pickett held brigade command under Longstreet early in the war, gaining praise for his limited service at Gaines Mill when a shoulder wound took him out of commission for subsequent campaigns. His elevation to division command was clearly due to Longstreet's fondness for him. "Long ringlets flowed loosely over his shoulders, trimmed and highly perfumed," as one of Longstreet's staff officers described Pickett, "his beard likewise was curling and giving out scents of Araby."[203]

Robert Ransom Jr., whose two-brigade division of North Carolinians was already slated to be transferred for duty in their native state at the start of the new year, had graduated from West Point in 1850. Although in temporary command of the division, Ransom retained direct command of his own brigade.[204]

Unlike Jackson and his division commanders, Longstreet maintained congenial relations with his subordinates, especially McLaws, Anderson and Pickett. Not only did Longstreet, McLaws and Anderson graduate from West Point in the same class and fought in the Mexican-American War, Longstreet's relationship with McLaws also extended back to their boyhood days in Georgia. Anderson's presence probably reminded Longstreet of his own South Carolina origins, while Pickett served as a link to Longstreet's first major experience in combat.

The time was 10:00 a.m. when French's division formed in preparation for its attack. Brigadier General Nathan Kimball commanded the lead brigade, which was also the strongest, with seven regiments. Colonel Oliver H. Palmer's three-regiment brigade formed two hundred yards behind, with Colonel John W. Andrews's Brigade of three regiments forming a line of battle two hundred yards behind Palmer. Three regiments—the Fourth Ohio, Eighth Ohio and First Delaware under the command of Colonel John S. Mason of the Eighth Ohio—would lead Kimball's advance three hundred yards in front as heavy skirmishers and drive out Confederates on the opposite side of the millrace to the foot of Marye's Heights. Additionally,

Mason's tiny command was to clear the plain of wooden fences and other obstacles, as well as clear outlying buildings of enemy sharpshooters in preparation of Kimball's attack.

Mason's men moved out at the double-quick about 11:00 a.m. As the men neared the eastern bank of the millrace, Confederate sharpshooters and artillery fire from one of the Washington Artillery batteries created some of the first casualties in the Federal ranks. Quickly routing the remaining Confederates, the Federal column crossed the millrace, where some of the men were bogged down knee-deep in water attempting to form a line for the continued advance. Braving the heavy fire, portions of the Eighth Ohio made their way to the Stratton family home and adjacent wheelwright shop and the Sisson Family grocery store, some of the few buildings on the edge of town. Lieutenant Colonel Franklin Sawyer, commanding the Eighth, recalled that this was "the last line of cover we could secure, and immediately in front of a strong line of stone wall that no skirmish line could carry." Sawyer's men halted their advance and took cover. Captain William P. Seville of the First Delaware, just south of the Eighth Ohio, recalled that his men advanced "through a perfect storm of bullets, shot, and shell" before seeking any shelter that could be found on the plain.[205]

The rest of Nathan Kimball's Brigade sprung forward with fixed bayonets and raced for Marye's Heights. Coming under heavy Confederate fire as they advanced, Kimball's men began losing their momentum as some stopped to return fire, while others lost steam once they traversed the four hundred yards to reach where Mason's skirmishers continued to hold their ground. Now these exposed troops were close enough to come under the fire of Cobb's Georgians behind the stone wall at the foot of Marye's Heights, yielding heavy casualties. Kimball received a wound, with command falling on the shoulders of Colonel Mason of the initial skirmishers. Andrew's Brigade, followed by Palmer's, entered into the fray, encountering a similar fate as Kimball. Forced to lie prone amid the storm of shell and shot from Marye's Heights, French's Division lost the strength to surge forward and take the Confederate position. "General French's line, before it reached us, was utterly broken, and the few men of the broken organization that reached out line at once sought shelter behind the houses and garden fences," remembered Colonel Sawyer of the 8th Ohio. One officer of the 132nd Pennsylvania simply stated, "Our men were being swept away by a terrific whirlwind."[206]

The members of the Washington Artillery on Marye's Heights and Willis Hill, augmented by Cobb's Georgia infantrymen posted below in the

Sunken Road and behind the stone wall, were the primary contributors to French's dilemma. Running low of small arms ammunition through their well-directed and rapid volleys, Cobb asked for support. Robert Ransom, whose North Carolina division was posted behind Marye's Heights, as well as the Twenty-fourth North Carolina on Cobb's left in the Sunken Road, quickly accommodated the Georgia brigadier's request. Although Cobb's brigade was part of McLaws's Division, Ransom believed that he held total command of the Marye's Heights sector of the Confederate line since the majority of his troops held the position and he was a ranking brigadier general in division command. Protocol in rank and unit organization did not seem to be a factor when emergencies arose for the Confederates on Marye's Heights. The same could not be said for the Federals farther south at Prospect Hill.[207]

Couch, viewing French's progress from the edge of town, wanted his division to carry the Confederate works at all costs. Ordering Hancock's Division forward, the II Corps commander hoped that these reinforcements could minimize French's casualties and renew the attack. Couch also ordered artillery support from the II Corps batteries posted at the edge of town. Due to the Federal artillerymen's difficulty in locating clear lines of sight, as well as their exposure to Confederate shells, their fire proved ineffective, mainly slamming into the buildings atop Willis Hill and Marye's Heights and achieving few Confederate casualties.[208]

One Federal shell did find its mark at the home of Martha Stephens next to the Sunken Road and just forward of the stone wall that served as Cobb's brigade headquarters. The fateful shell burst against the house, splintering into pieces, with one of them breaking the bone and severing the femoral artery of General Cobb's right thigh above the knee. Moments earlier, Brigadier General John R. Cooke of Ransom's Division had been struck in the forehead by a Federal bullet after conferring with Cobb in bringing his North Carolinians down from Marye's Heights to reinforce the stone wall. Cooke would later recover from his wound. Thomas Cobb was taken behind the lines, where he died later that day. Upon Cobb's wounding, McLaws dispatched Brigadier General Joseph B. Kershaw's South Carolina brigade from its position near Lee's Hill to the south to support Cobb's men and so that Kershaw himself could assume command of the Sunken Road sector.[209]

Winfield Scott Hancock had hoped to expand the Federal attack area in his efforts to reinforce French. Unfortunately, French's Division had lost its steam as his men either sought protection for their very survival in a swale on the open plain parallel to the Sunken Road or were completely withdrawing

COBB'S AND KERSHAW'S TROOPS BEHIND THE STONE WALL.

Above: A sketch of Confederate soldiers behind a stone wall, paralleling the Telegraph (Sunken) Road, repelling the repeated Federal assaults. The small house on the right is the Innis House. *Library of Congress.*

Left: Brigadier General Thomas R.R. Cobb (1823–1862) commanded a Georgia brigade behind the stone wall before being mortally wounded by shrapnel by a Federal artillery shell. Battles and Leaders of the Civil War, *vol. 3.*

back into Fredericksburg. Hancock briefed his brigade commanders with the simplified orders that if the leading brigade faltered, then the one behind would take up the advance until the enemy works were carried. Hancock's Division formed up at the edge of town with Colonel Samuel K. Zook's six-regiment brigade made up of units from Connecticut, Delaware, New York and Pennsylvania. Behind Zook was the famed "Irish Brigade" commanded by the Emerald Isle's expatriate Brigadier General Thomas F. Meagher. His five units contained first-generation Irish, as well as Irish Americans of the 28th Massachusetts, 63rd New York, 66th New York, 88th New York and the 116th Pennsylvania. Third in line was the brigade of Brigadier General John C. Caldwell, consisting of three regiments from New York, two from Pennsylvania and one from New Hampshire.

Hancock's men formed in the midst of a lull in the Confederate artillery barrage atop the heights. Their two main obstacles were negotiating the torn-down fences and planks placed in the plain by Cobb's men days before to hinder the progress of a Federal attack and French's men streaming through their own ranks to the safety of Fredericksburg. An officer in the Twenty-seventh Connecticut remembered that "Hancock, rode slowly and proudly up and down the line, surveying the ranks, his countenance wearing an aspect of quiet and cool determination." When the division commander reached the Twenty-seventh, he reminded them, "You are the only Connecticut regiment in my division. Bring no dishonor upon the State you represent."

Zook's brigade charged amid revived shelling from the Confederate batteries. "A shell would strike in a body of men," Sergeant Gilbert Frederick of the Fifty-seventh New York related, "and fill the air with pieces of flesh, clothing, and accoutrements." Federal batteries opened up from the other side of the Rappahannock in support of Hancock's assault, only to fall short of the heights and cause casualties in the Federal ranks. Couch immediately ordered these long-range batteries to cease fire. The right of Caldwell's line reached the bricked Stratton House, with the various regiments intermingled as the enemy fire increased in intensity. The young Connecticut officer and his comrades were within one hundred yards of the stone wall, only to be stymied by the Georgians and North Carolinians behind the wall rising up and firing well-placed volleys into the Federal ranks. "[T]he men remained at this point the rest of the afternoon," the Connecticut officer related, "loading their guns on the ground, then rising sufficiently to deliver their fire." Sergeant Frederick and the men of the Fifty-seventh New York charging to the left of the Stratton House pulled their hats over their eyes and leaned forward "as if breasting a storm" when they came within Confederate rifle range. Frederick claimed that members of the Fifty-seventh held position on a slight knoll thirty yards from the stone wall for several hours. Several of Zook's regiments were running low on ammunition, and Hancock ordered Meagher's Irish Brigade to go in.

Private William McCarter of the 116th Pennsylvania had already heard the news from one of his officers about French's previous assault. "Well, boys, French is licked, to beat Hell," the officer related to McCarter and his comrades. "We are soon to go over the same ground and try the same job that he failed to accomplish…Keep cool and do your duty when brought face to face with the enemy." Zook's brigade had already faced the enemy, and Hancock soon personally escorted Meagher's brigade to the millrace. The brigade commander had distributed green springs of boxwood to be stuck in the caps of the men of the brigade as "emblems of Erin's nationality." Once over the canal and already having suffered casualties, the Irish Brigade reformed with bayonets fixed. As the brigade reached about fifty paces from the stone wall, according to McCarter, the Confederates "suddenly sprang up from behind it where they had been entirely concealed from our view till that moment." Meagher's men were stopped cold. "It was simply madness to advance as far as we did," McCarter surmised, "and an utter impossibility to go forward." The bodies of the dead and wounded also became serious obstacles for further advance. One of Meagher's staff officers recounted, "Some broke for the rear, others lay down among the dead."

Caldwell's brigade was poised to make an attack in the wake of the Irish Brigade's ill-fated assault. Advancing left to right with the 145th Pennsylvania, 7th New York, 81st Pennsylvania and 5th New Hampshire, Caldwell led his men forward. Forming up behind this front line were the 61st and 64th New York Regiments, consolidated under Colonel Nelson A. Miles, one of Hancock's more aggressive field commanders. Passing along the length of his line, Caldwell urged his men forward while he kept men in the rear ranks from accidently firing into the backs of their comrades in the front ranks. Passing beyond the Stratton House, Caldwell reported that his men experienced a terrific fire "the hottest I have ever seen," which thinned his ranks rapidly. Colonel Miles, eager to lead a charge to gain the works, requested permission to do so. "Had there been any support," Caldwell later wrote, "I should not have hesitated to give him the order to do so." Both Hancock and Caldwell were fearful of a Confederate counterattack on the right of their position. Elements of Zook's Brigade had earlier encountered the 24th North Carolina posted north of Cobb's Brigade. Caldwell dispatched Miles and his New York command to hold the right flank of the Federal position. By the time Miles reached his command, he was struck by a bullet in the throat.[210]

Darius Couch, by this time, had left his position at the edge of town for a better view of the battlefield: the cupola of the circuit courthouse on Princess Anne Street. Joining him was O.O. Howard, commanding his last division yet to be deployed. "Oh, great God! See how our men, our poor fellows are falling!" Couch lamented. Receiving Hancock's urgent request for reinforcements, Couch ordered Howard to abandon his position guarding the upper portion of Fredericksburg and "work in on the right" of Hancock. Saunders Piatt's three-regiment brigade was detached from Stoneman's III Corps of Hooker's Center Grand Division to guard the upper parts of the city as Howard prepared for his assault. On his way to battle, Howard encountered a group of soldiers carrying an officer with a neck wound from the field, revealed to be one of his former staff officers: Colonel Nelson A. Miles. "Seated on a stretcher and holding the lips of the wound together," Howard wrote, "[Miles] pluckily had himself brought to me to show where he thought I could put my troops into action to advantage so as to make some impression on the enemy's line." Sumner, still staying put at the Lacy House across the river, concurred with Couch's troop dispositions and ordered Orlando Willcox to advance Brigadier General Samuel D. Sturgis's IX Corps division to the left of Couch's men. It was hoped that Howard's three brigades and Sturgis's two brigades could coordinate their movements along with the remnants of the commands of French and Hancock to carry the works.

Howard reached the edge of town slightly north of the first two divisional assaults, ordering Colonel Joshua T. Owen's four Pennsylvania regiments (dubbed the "Philadelphia Brigade") forward, to be followed by Colonel Norman J. Hall's brigade. Brigadier General Alfred Sully's Brigade would act as a reserve. Owen deployed south of Hanover Street and advanced toward the direction of the Stratton House. Hall crossed the millrace, positioning his brigade north of Hanover Street. Hall, with Sully's brigade close behind, would be the first Federal units in a position to potentially

A sketch of the Federal assaults against Marye's Heights, possibly from the vantage point of the circuit courthouse cupola. This would have been the view of the battlefield of Generals Couch, Willcox and Howard. *Waud, Library of Congress.*

flank Ransom's Division in the Sunken Road. "My regiments began to fire when each in its turn reached the general line of battle," Howard recalled. Hall's flanking advantage was neutralized by enfilading artillery fire from the Donaldson (Louisiana) Artillery on the northern end of Marye's Heights. Much of Howard's attack consisted of piecemeal assaults by portions of his brigades. Howard's men survivng the assaults sought the shelter of a nearby tannery.

Ransom had committed all of his men to the defense of the heights and the Sunken Road just as Kershaw arrived at the head of two of his South Carolina regiments from behind the Willis Hill Cemetery. The South Carolinian found that "[t]he position was excellent." The rest of his command was not far behind. D. Augustus Dickert of the Third South Carolina recalled that Kershaw ordered his arriving regiments "to double-up with Cobb's men, and to hold their position 'at the sacrifice of every man of their commands.'" Several of Kershaw's men became casualties to Federal shelling from the edge of town and across the river as they marched across the crest of the heights, exposing themselves while getting into position near the Sunken Road.[211]

Coordination between Howard's Division on the right and Sturgis's Division on the left would not materialize. Pennsylvanian Samuel Davis Sturgis was a member of the famous West Point class of 1846 and was a Mexican-American War veteran serving in the U.S. Dragoons and Cavalry. He had been in command of his division since the Battle of South Mountain in Maryland. It had taken some time for Sturgis to get his two brigades readied for the attack, and Howard's advance had already stalled by then. Brigadier General Edward Ferrero, a New York City dancing instructor, commanded one of Sturgis's brigades that formed four of its regiments near the railroad depot at the southern end of town. Ferrero's men headed straight toward the fairgrounds that occupied a large portion of the open plain leading to the Sunken Road. "Keep cool," he reassured his men, "it is good fun when you once get in!" Leander Cogswell of the Eleventh New Hampshire saw the enemy's artillery "belch forth long sheets of flame." Charles Walcott of the Twenty-first Massachusetts witnessed the destructive power of the Confederate shells "when the head of tall Warren Webster...flew from his shoulders, and while the horrid red fountain was still spouting from the neck" as the entire line was ordered forward.

A high board fence halted the advance, and Ferrero's men had difficulty tearing it down. Most of the troops were able to get through small tears in the fence, but such passages were "blocked up with heaps of dead, dying, and wounded, who had to be trampled upon in order to get through," according to Thomas Parker of the Fifty-first Pennsylvania. Parker recalled how his fellow Pennsylvanians fell "at every step, some killed outright, some with a leg or an arm torn off, some with their bowels or brains oozing out." No sympathy was given to the skulkers who fell "as if they had been hit, but in fact had only fallen to impress their officers that they had been wounded, thus escape proceeding further." Portions of Ferrero's brigade connected with the left portion of Howard's division near the Stratton House. The number of Federal troops lying prone in the large swale in mud paralleling the Confederate position in the Sunken Road continued to grow into an uncoordinated mass. Running low on ammunition, Ferrero personally requested Sturgis to release his remaining regiment—the Fifty-first New York—that had been supporting an artillery battery earlier in the day. Granted the request, the New Yorkers left their position in a nearby brickyard to reinforce their brigade. Accompanying the regiment was their mascot, a large black dog who "seemed to be aware of the danger of the place." Crouching low on the ground with the soldiers, the dog was able to avoid the shells saturating the plain. In the attempt to change position, the unfortunate canine was hit by a ball, and "he sank down to rise no more."

Brigadier General James Nagle commanded the other brigade of Sturgis's Division. Five of his six regiments had been ordered to support Ferrero but did not reach the battlefield in a cohesive fashion. Reaching the edge of town south of Frederick Street, Nagle's men shifted their formation in a very loose fashion somewhat parallel to an unfinished western spur of the Richmond, Fredericksburg and Potomac Railroad. While the Seventh Rhode Island and Sixth New Hampshire forming Nagle's right came in line with Ferrero's men, the Second Maryland, Twelfth Rhode Island and Ninth New Hampshire on the left were positioned at an angle close to the base of Willis Hill and were coming under heavy Confederate fire from the Washington Artillery on Willis Hill and Confederate batteries farther south on Telegraph (Lee's) Hill.

Seeking safety from enemy artillery, the left of Nagle's line sought safety in the unfinished railroad cut, splitting the brigade. Unfortunately for these Federals, the enemy batteries had drawn perfect aim on them and unleashed a constant barrage of shot and shell. "There was no retreat," one Ninth New Hampshire veteran reminiscence; "to remain there was death, and to go forward…there was the same murderous fire of artillery, combined with that of infantry." As the soldiers emerged from the cut to join the general fighting on the plain, they were met with a shower of bullets. "The ground was strewn with dead and wounded and debris of all sorts," recalled Oscar Lapham of the Twelfth Rhode Island. The right portion of Nagle's brigade surged forward, only to be bogged down by the mix of Federal troops lying prone in the mud-soaked plain. "The boys hugged mother earth that afternoon," recalled an officer in the Sixth New Hampshire. "They could not turn over to fire without exposing themselves." The Forty-eighth Pennsylvania of Nagle's Brigade had been held in reserve along Frederick Street and advanced over the field to relieve the Twenty-first Massachusetts of Fererro's brigade running out of ammunition. When the men of the Forty-eighth reached the main battle line, they all lay flat on the muddy ground. Litters and stretchers of wounded were being carried to the rear, and in one instance members of the Forty-eighth had to make way. One soldier failed to heed the orders of Major James Wren and remained still. Wren punched the disobedient soldier, but to no avail. "[H]e lay Quiet & made no reply," Wren recorded in his diary, "& when we examined him, he was dead as neat."[212]

Brigadier General Samuel D. Sturgis (1822–1889), commanding the Second Division, IX Corps, led the fourth major assault against Marye's Heights. *Library of Congress.*

Couch had committed his entire corps in three costly assaults, while Willcox contributed a fourth, with Sturgis's division leaving approximately 4,798 Federal casualties on the field. Sumner's Right Grand Division was nowhere near dislodging Longstreet's Confederates from the heights behind Fredericksburg.[213]

About the time that Sturgis's Division prepared its advance toward Willis Hill and Marye's Heights, both Meade and Gibbon were withdrawing their divisions after failing to sustain and follow up Meade's breakthrough on Jackson's lines farther south. Burnside sent a staff officer to Franklin, ordering him to renew his attacks on Prospect Hill, believing that the latter officer would use his own initiative in complying with this directive. The proximity of Burnside's army headquarters at the Gothic Revival–styled Phillips House almost two miles behind Sumner's headquarters at the Lacy House probably compelled the army commander to focus his immediate efforts on seizing Marye's Heights. Besides, Franklin had two III Corps divisions from Hooker's Center Grand Division on hand, and his expected success in the sector of the battlefield promised hope for a Federal victory. Or so Burnside hoped.

Hooker, whom Burnside distrusted, still had the entire V Corps of his Center Grand Division available to reinforce Sumner's troops to capitalize on Franklin's anticipated

Brigadier General Charles Griffin (1825–1867), commanding the First Division, V Corps of Hooker's Center Grand Division, led the fifth major assault against Marye's Heights. *Library of Congress.*

success. Brigadier General Charles Griffin's V Corps division crossed the pontoons into Fredericksburg in the early afternoon of December 13 to bolster the IX Corps. Likewise, the remaining brigade of Brigadier General Amiel W. Whipple's III Corps division under Colonel Samuel S. Carroll stationed in Fredericksburg was ordered as reinforcements for the IX Corps.

Griffin, an experienced and battle-hardened artillery battery commander, had initially moved into position to support Sturgis's division stalled below Marye's Heights. It became clear that Sturgis was unable to renew his assault, and Griffin's troops ended up relieving Sturgis's men and prepared for their own assault on the Confederate works. Carroll, reporting to Willcox with his small brigade, received orders to form to the left of Sturgis. "I immediately moved out to obey the order," Carroll later reported, "but the head of my column came in contact with General Griffin's division, which seemed to be moving to the support of General Sturgis, and I joined it, moved abreast of one of his brigades into the railroad cut, and, finding I could move no farther without breaking that column, halted there while it filed off to the left." Although Carroll was willing to take his orders from Griffin as the senior on-scene battlefield commander, Griffin was unaware of Carroll's presence, and Willcox was perplexed as to why Carroll had not charged forward.

In spite of the command confusion, Carroll and his men with fixed bayonets made a dash toward the enemy works before crashing into the portions of Colonel Jacob Sweitzer's Brigade of Griffin's Division at the unfinished railroad cut. Yielding the right-of-way to two of Griffin's brigades, Carroll joined Sweitzer's Brigade and Colonel James Barnes's Brigade to begin the fifth Federal assault to take Marye's Heights. One officer in the 118th Pennsylvania recalled seeing numerous Federal soldiers from the previous unsuccessful attacks ahead of the advance who had thrown themselves on the ground to avoid the Confederate artillery and small arms fire. "[T]hey were too proud to retreat," he wrote, "and there they were, hundreds, thousands of them, in plain view, flat on their faces." The young officer made a later, horrifying discovery: "Will you believe it—they were dead, all dead men that I saw, but did not know it at the time." Griffin's two brigades along with Carroll's were hit hard by the continuous Confederate shelling.

Griffin, who had received a wound but refused to leave the field, ordered in his last brigade under Colonel Thomas B.W. Stockton. Captain Eugene A. Nash of the Forty-fourth New York in Stockton's Brigade explained "our experience was the same that befell those who had preceded us." Broken ranks continued forward as the air "filled with shot, bursting shells, and the deadly minnies." As the ranks closed and continued farther, they soon became broken again. "The wounded and dying," Nash continued, "sank together on the blood-soaked field." Stockton's men had reached the farthest limit of the previous assaults and sought refuge in any depression and swale on the muddy field that could found. Griffin lost about 926 men to casualties in the assault, while Carroll's brigade had 111 for its efforts.[214]

In the wake of Griffin's attack, Burnside received information that Franklin had not renewed the assaults, as ordered, after the repulses of Meade and Gibbon. He repeated his order to Franklin for an all-out attack on the Confederate positions south of Fredericksburg. The army commander was not aware that his Left Grand Division commander had been shaken by the failure to capitalize on the breakthrough of A.P. Hill's lines, as well as from aggressive Confederate actions near Deep Run. Franklin, not understanding his primary role in Burnside's battle plans, sought to maintain a defensive posture for the duration.

Meanwhile, Burnside ordered Hooker to send in the remaining two divisions of the V Corps to support the beleaguered II Corps troops in front of Marye's Heights. Renewed offensives on both fronts held the promise of victory in Burnside's mind. Sumner sent a dispatch to Couch: "Hooker has been ordered to put in everything. You must hold on until he comes." A relieved Couch likened Hooker's reinforcements to "the breaking out of the sun in a storm."

Hooker rode into Fredericksburg to survey the scene that awaited some of the troops of his Center Grand Division. He had already received reports of high Federal casualties in that sector of the battlefield and anticipated that his own troops would have a supporting role with regard to Couch's troops. Conferring with Couch and his division commanders, the normally aggressive Hooker realized that further assaults would be costly and personally rode to Burnside's headquarters two miles distant to plead with the army commander to suspend any further attacks. An insistent Burnside ordered Hooker's divisions to take the heights behind Fredericksburg. Orders at 4:00

The Washington Artillery of New Orleans in action on Marye's Heights. *Battles and Leaders of the Civil War, vol. 3.*

Confederate defensive positions on Willis Hill. *National Archives.*

p.m. had already been issued for Brigadier General Andrew A. Humphreys's V Corps division of raw Pennsylvania troops to make a sixth assault to carry Marye's Heights.[215]

The Confederate batteries of the Washington Artillery had been hammering away at the Federal attacks for the better part of five hours and were running dangerously low on ammunition. At about 3:30 p.m., Colonel Walton had sent an urgent note to Lieutenant Colonel Alexander for relief of his guns. Alexander, in his first battle commanding troops, decided not to replenish the Washington Artillery's ammunition but to replace its guns with those of his own command. Gathering up nine guns from Woolfolk's, Jordan's and Moody's Batteries, Alexander started for Marye's Heights under severe enemy artillery fire and with difficulty in negotiating his teams on the road, where their dead comrades continued to lay. As the Washington Artillery pulled out of position, the relief would not be in position for a few minutes, giving a moment of grief for the Confederate high command and a moment of hope for the Federal high command.

Lee and Longstreet, observing the removal of Walton's guns from atop Telegraph Hill to the south, sent immediate orders for the Washington Artillery to stay put until they observed Alexander's guns going into action. The slacking of Confederate artillery convinced Hooker—back in Fredericksburg and the ranking general on the field—to order forward the II Corps artillery batteries to bombard the heights and possibly blow a breach directly into the stone wall in preparation of another assault attempt. One of the several batteries brought forward was Battery B, First Rhode Island Light Artillery, under Captain John G. Hazard. "Our position was a perfect hornet's nest," recalled Acting Corporal John H. Rhodes of the battery, "with the hornets all stirred up." Exposed to enemy fire in one of the most dangerous areas of the field, Hazard's Battery continued to blaze away for almost an hour when the order to cease fire was given to make way for Humphreys's Division when the Federal general saw Walton's batteries leave their position on Marye's Heights.[216]

Humphreys, a West Point graduate and a prewar army topographical engineer, commanded a two-brigade division of 4,500 men who were to experience their first major combat. "My troops were yet in the act of forming…when I received an urgent request from Major General Couch to support that part of his corps on the left of the Telegraph road, and almost at the same moment a staff officer rode up and informed him that General Griffin would re-enforce him," Humphreys reported. Both Hooker and Couch agreed that direct frontal assaults were fruitless and sought to operate on the right of the Federal line, hitting the Confederate position north of the extension of Hanover Street as it ran past the Sunken Road. Humphreys had initially positioned the four-regiment brigade of Colonel Peter H. Allanbach into such a position. Realizing that Marye's Heights would have to be taken by the point of the bayonet and that a nearby ravine offered the best vantage point for launching an attack, Humphreys shifted Allanbach's men south of the Hanover Street extension. Allanbach's Brigade advanced toward the stone wall, belying the "romantic image of unbroken lines of soldiers marching shoulder to shoulder" depicted in contemporary drawings, as historian Carol Reardon has noted. The uneven terrain, irregular fence lines and enemy obstacles that stymied prior assaults affected these Pennsylvanians. Alexander's fresh artillery on the heights and tightly packed infantry behind the stone wall, up to three or four ranks deep, caused Allanbach's efforts to melt away.

The increased intensity of Confederate fire killed or disabled the majority of horses ridden by Humprheys's staff officers, including his own. Borrowing a mount, the division commander retrieved his second four-regiment brigade of Pennsylvanians under Brigadier General Erastus B. Tyler. "I rode to General Tyler's brigade to conduct it to the enemy," Humphreys stated, "and while doing so received three successive orders from General Butterfield to charge the enemy's line, the last order being accompanied by the message that both General Burnside and General Hooker demanded that the crest should be taken before night." Tyler's Brigade encountered its first obstacle in the form of the guns of Hazard's Rhode Island Battery and Battery G, First New York Light Artillery, under Captain John D. Frank, blocking their advance as they dueled with Alexander's batteries on the heights. Once Tyler was able to resume his advance, his brigade tramping across the muddy field was halted temporarily by masses of prone Federal troops, discouraging their attack. In spite of the personal bravery of Humprhreys and Tyler—exposing themselves on horseback to a murderous enemy fire and encouraging their men forward—Tyler's attack stalled, and the men sought protection behind the Stratton House and Sisson's Store as sunlight gave way to darkness. For all of his efforts, Humprhreys had more than one thousand casualties and had the highest percentage of casualties of any of the assaulting divisions

Brigadier General Daniel Butterfield commanded the V Corps, Center Grand Division, Army of the Potomac. Two of his divisions participated in the assaults against Marye's Heights. *Library of Congress.*

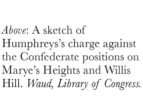

Above: A sketch of Humphreys's charge against the Confederate positions on Marye's Heights and Willis Hill. *Waud, Library of Congress.*

Right: Brigadier General Andrew A. Humphreys (1810–1883), commanding the Third Division, V Corps, led Pennsylvania troops in the sixth major assault against Marye's Heights. *Library of Congress.*

against Marye's Heights. The attempts at capturing the heights were fast becoming forlorn hopes.[217]

In support of Humphreys's attack, Willcox ordered one of his IX Corps divisions under Brigadier General George W. Getty to hit the Confederate position on its right, similar to Sturgis's earlier attack. Getty's two brigades under Colonels Rush C. Hawkins and Edward Harland sent their commands forward from the position of the railroad and into the unfinished railroad cut. As darkness began to descend on Mayre's Heights, Hawkins emerged from the railroad cut leading Connecticut, Rhode Island, New Hampshire and New York men in an exchange of small arms fire with North and South Carolinians on the southern end of the stone wall. Confusion in the darkness, thickening mud, dead and dying Federal soldiers on the field and a steady barrage of Confederate fire halted Getty's efforts by six o'clock that evening. "The attack of our division closed a battle which was one of the most disastrous defeats to the Union forces during the war," wrote Hawkins after the war, "The sadness which prevailed throughout the whole army on that night can neither be described nor imagined." Hooker, in virtual command of the final assaults, reported a week after Fredericksburg to members of the Joint Committee on the Conduct of the War, "Finding that I lost as many men as my orders required me to lose, I suspended the attack."

Longstreet reinforced the Marye's Heights sector of his lines with Brigadier General James L. Kemper's Virginia Brigade from Pickett's Division. His First Corps totaled 1,511 Confederate casualties for the day. Sumner's and Hooker's participating units reported 7,480 casualties, mingled with a higher number of unhurt survivors, in a one-and-a-half-mile swath, left out on the open plain in front of the stone wall below Marye's Heights—giving the fighting here the appropriate and rightful designation as the Slaughter of Fredericksburg.[218]

Chapter 6

It Is Well that War Is So Terrible

The Aftermath of Fredericksburg

At the height of the Federal assaults against Marye's Heights on December 13, 1862, Confederate commander Robert E. Lee and his subordinate, James Longstreet, surveyed the unfolding scene through their field glasses from Lee's headquarters atop Telegraph Hill. From this vantage point, Lee saw the steady lines of blue-clad infantry decimated by the shot and shell hurled forth by the guns of the Washington Artillery of Longstreet's Corps. Yet the enemy continued to surge forward again and again, doomed to certain death and destruction. "It is well that war is so terrible," Lee said turning to Longstreet, "we should grow too fond of it." The rush of intestinal fortitude on both sides displaying bravery and courage subsided with the termination of hostilities ushering in the stark reality of war and its consequences. "Fredericksburg is not a pleasant topic for a Union soldier," said Augustus Buell, a veteran of Battery B, Fourth U.S. Artillery, almost three decades after the battle. Burnside accumulated 12,653 casualties while Lee only lost 4,909 at Fredericksburg.[219]

Lieutenant Nathan T. Bartley of the Seventh Virginia in Kemper's Brigade, relieving some of Ransom's troops in the Sunken Road behind the stone wall, recalled watching Federals removing the wounded from their front. "[T]he crys [sic] and groans and prayers of those poor fellows in the death-like stillness of the night you know must have awakened within us thoughts like these that the glories of war one gained at a dreadful sacrifice." Hardened veterans of Antietam could not fathom the experience before them. One Confederate in the Fourth Georgia of D.H. Hill's Division was "arrested by the groans of a wounded man" who he soon discovered was the very Federal soldier who had "tenderly nursed him" when he had been wounded on the field at Antietam. Later exchanged and rejoining his regiment in time for Fredericksburg, the Georgia soldier sought permission from his brigade commander to remove the wounded foe from the field who in granting the request "charged him to take special care of his friend, and nurse him until he got well." A soldier in the Eighth Georgia of Hood's Division on picket duty on the evening of December 13 could hear the cries of wounded Yankees in the nearby swamp. "I was very ancious [sic] to assist them," he wrote, "but it was against positive orders to go in the swamp so they had to lay there all night." Captain Dickert of the Third South Carolina recalled the "piteous calls for help and water" that he thought "were simply heart-rending." Several soldiers from Kershaw's Brigade made individual excursions in the darkness beyond the stone wall, braving both friendly and enemy fire to render comfort to suffering wounded Federal soldiers.[220]

John Haley of the Seventeenth Maine in front of Prospect Hill that evening worried for his wounded comrades left behind on the field to the mercies of the weather and Rebels. "These wretched men lay crying, groaning, and begging for water and help in the most agonizing manner, and we were unable to rescue them," Haley recounted sadly. "The rustle of a leaf or the cracking of a twig might send a shower of Rebel bullets into our ranks." Colonel Rush C. Hawkins, who led some of the last troops against Marye's Heights, believed that "[t]he surgeons were the happiest of all, for they were so busy that they had no time to think of our terrible defeat."

For many of the Federal soldiers, the ambulances had not yet reached them to carry them to the surgeons' operating tables. Lieutenant Colonel Joshua Chamberlain of the Twentieth Maine in Griffin's Division, lying prone on the open plain in the darkness, had to keep warm between two dead soldiers killed in earlier assaults since his regiment had discarded their overcoats and knapsacks prior to going into battle. "Necessity compels strange uses," he remarked. Moved by the cries for water, names of loved ones called out in delirium or the requests for quick death, Chamberlain and the regimental adjutant left their safer position to see what they could do to help "these forsaken sufferers." Chamberlain remembered after the war:

We did what we could, but how little it was on a field so boundless for feeble human reach! Our best was to search the canteens of the dead for a draft of water for the dying; or to ease the posture of a broken limb; or to compress a severed artery of fast-ebbing life that might perhaps so be saved, with what little skill we had been taught by our surgeons early in learning the tactics of saving as well as of destroying men. It was a place and time for farewells. Many a word was taken for far-away homes that otherwise might never have had one token from the field of the lost. It was something even to let the passing spirit know that its worth was not forgotten here.

Relief finally came when "the dusky forms of ghostly ambulances gliding up on the far edge of the field" arrived to collect the wounded.[221]

The Federals and Confederates had heroes on both sides tending and making attempts to tend to the wounded. Perhaps the most well-known story of heroism on the Fredericksburg Battlefield was that of nineteen-year-old Sergeant Richard Rowland Kirkland of the Second South Carolina. Hearing the cries of the Federal wounded in front of the stone wall and maybe motivated by some of his fellow Confederates assisting wounded foes, Kirkland asked his brigade commander General Joseph Kershaw for permission to give water to the wounded soldiers under a white flag of truce. Kershaw could not grant Kirkland such protection since no general truce had been negotiated, leaving both sides that evening in a hostile posture. Understanding the sincerity of the young soldier's mission of mercy, Kershaw could only wish him well if he chose to proceed. Gathering as many canteens filled with water at the Stephens House well that he could possibly carry, Kirkland braved potential fire from both sides spending a few hours giving water to wounded enemy soldiers, placing knapsacks under their heads and making them as comfortable as possible. The young South Carolinian was bestowed the title the "Angel of Marye's Heights" for his heroic efforts that cold and miserable evening in December.[222]

The full impact of the Federal repulse had not gained full possession of Burnside's sense of reality. Holding a council of war with his grand division commanders in the early morning hours of December 14, the army commander prepared orders for his old IX Corps to renew the assaults against Marye's Heights. Burnside would lead them personally in the attack. His chief subordinates objected to the new plan that bordered on personal suicide on the part of Burnside, with Hooker's denunciations bordering on insubordination. Franklin apparently approached Bursnide later that morning suggesting a renewed attack on Jackson's lines, but Burnside declined, probably having lost faith in his subordinate for failing to carry out his orders and seeking some personal vindication in leading troops against the stone wall. Burnside rode into Fredericksburg to confer with the corps, division and brigade commanders, who gave their stark and frank assessment of the Army of the Potomac's situation. Returning to his headquarters at the Phillips House, Burnside continued with his plans, ordering Sumner to prepare orders for the IX Corps. By the next morning, several Federal generals had gathered at army headquarters to persuade Burnside to suspend the attack. By 10:00 a.m. that morning, Sumner, who had supported all of Burnside's decisions, made a personal appeal to his chief to not go forward with his plan. Reality began to set in on Ambrose Burnside.

Later that day, II Corps commander Darius Couch encountered Burnside. Couch assured him that his men had done all that they could, as he would later report that they had shown "such determined courage as in this day's fight against stone wall, rifle-pits, and enfilading batteries." According to Couch, Burnside replied in a cheerful-sounding tone, "Couch, I know that; I am perfectly satisfied that you did your best." But Couch believed that Burnside harbored personal guilt that he had led his army into a disaster "and one knowing him so long and well as myself could see that he wished his body was also lying in front of Marye's Heights." Couch claimed that he had never felt so bad for any man in his life. The commander of the VI Corps, William "Baldy" Smith, received what could be considered a natural response from Burnside when he encountered him in his tent alone pacing back and forth "dazed by the defeat and grief-stricken at the loss of life." According to Smith's recollections, Burnside turned to him and cried, "'Oh! those men! oh! those men!' I asked what he meant, and he said, 'Those men over there!' pointing across the river where so many thousands lay dead and wounded, 'I am thinking of them all the time.'" Smith also asserted in his postwar reminiscences that Burnside revealed his intention to relieve Sumner from duty, arrest Hooker and recommend Franklin for army command.[223]

The Army of Northern Virginia, unable to prod the Federals into an attack, continued to improve its defensive positions for much of December 14. The following day, a temporary truce was called to allow Burnside's ambulances to collect wounded lying in the fields for the better part of two days without fear of being fired upon. One Virginia solider on Jackson's front wrote that the soldiers on both sides "entered into friendly converse, traded tobacco, coffee, and sugar. Night approached, and put a stop to this; and each man took his place in the line, ready to shoot the man in his front on sight!" Burnside, unable to persuade his commanders to renew the assaults, met with his grand division commanders and decided to keep a small force

Damaged buildings in Fredericksburg, possibly on the lower end of Caroline Street. Note the steeple of the Episcopal church to the far left on Princess Anne Street. *National Archives.*

under Hooker's direction occupying Fredericksburg and the bridgeheads while the rest of the army evacuated to the other side of the Rappahannock. Under the cover of darkness, the Army of the Potomac skillfully and swiftly withdrew from its position. In response to a preliminary report via telegram that Burnside sent to Washington, General Halleck encouraged the army commander to renew his attacks or at least hold his position on the Fredericksburg side of the river. By the early morning hours of December 16, Hooker reported to Burnside his concern over the fact that the small number of troops in his command holding Fredericksburg in the face of the enemy might not be sufficient to maintain a solid defense. Reluctantly, Burnside ordered the complete withdrawal of Federal troops.[224]

Late that same evening, and for several days after, a natural phenomenon occurred in the evening skies. As one member of the Sixteenth Mississippi recorded in his diary of a sighting on December 23:

> *Around 2 o'clock, darkness became as bright as day. Apparently it was dawn. But the light came from the west instead of the east. Strange. Then the light died out, flickering red again as it lighted the men's faces. The dawn was the Aurora Borealis—the Northern Lights—heaven itself setting off fireworks to celebrate our victory.*

When dawn of the sixteenth approached, Lee discovered to his disappointment that his army had indeed achieved a victory, with Burnside's troops giving up the field of battle. Unfortunately, the Federal dead had been left on the field. In an unprecedented move, Lee requested a truce with Burnside to allow the Federals to bury their fallen comrades. Longstreet's chief of staff, Major Sorrell, on his way to deliver the formal documents to Federal officers to commence the truce, made his way through Fredericksburg:

> *It was pitiful riding through the town, considerably damaged as it was by the artillery fire from Stafford Heights, but more still from the plundering and looting that had gone on while in possession of the United States troops. Furniture, bedding, mattresses, carpets, china, domestic utensils, indeed all that went to make up those comfortable old homes, were strewn helter skelter, broken and ruined about the streets. The streets were filled with distressed women and children, both black and white.*

Fredericksburg had suffered an ordeal that would take time to heal. Groups of Federal soldiers spent much of the day hastily burying their dead in mass trenches before returning to the other side of the river.[225]

"If there is a worse place than hell," Lincoln remarked upon confirmation of the disaster at Fredericksburg, "I am in it." Burnside's defeat caused Lincoln not only personal but also political distress. Moreover, Congressional leaders attempted to shake up his cabinet, causing both Secretary of State William H. Seward and Secretary of the Treasury Salmon P. Chase to submit their resignations to Lincoln, which he promptly rejected. Major General William S. Rosecrans's limited victory over General Braxton Bragg's Confederates at Stone's River (Murfreesboro) the following month did very little to mitigate the military failure of Ambrose Burnside at Fredericksburg and the unsuccessful joint effort of Major Generals Ulysses S. Grant and William T. Sherman to capture Vicksburg, Mississippi.

Meanwhile, the members of the Joint Committee on the Conduct of the War arrived at Aquia Landing on December 18, spending a day interviewing Burnside, Franklin, Sumner, Hooker and other key officers. It was clear from general testimonies that the delay of the pontoon bridges was a key factor in the eventual defeat of the Army of the Potomac. The committee members further explored Franklin's failure to follow the spirit of Burnside's intentions at Prospect Hill with a full-scale assault instead of following the strict letter of Burnside's (self-admitted) poorly worded orders. The mostly Republican committee needed a scapegoat for the

Federal failure at Fredericksburg, and William B. Franklin became their leading candidate given his identification with George McClellan and the Democratic Party. Interviews of Generals Halleck and Meigs in Washington concluded the early rounds of the committee's investigation. Franklin had come to the private conclusion that the Lincoln administration, and Halleck in particular, was the main cause for the defeat and that Burnside had been manipulated to serve political ends.

Burnside made a brief trip to Washington after his testimony before the Congressional committee, during which he showed Lincoln a letter he had composed to General Halleck (intended for the press) placing all responsibility for Fredericksburg on his shoulders. Lincoln, perhaps with a sigh of relief, assented to its publication. Publicly acknowledging that his movements from Warrenton were against the wishes of his superiors, Burnside plainly stated that "[f]or the failure in the attack, I am responsible, as the extreme gallantry, courage and endurance shown by them [Army of the Potomac] was never exceeded, and would have carried the points had it been possible."[226]

Lincoln, still believing in Burnside's loyalty and sincerity, awaited the bewhiskered general's next move. Burnside was already having his subordinates and engineers examine suitable crossings below Fredericksburg. His intentions were to send William W. Averell's cavalry brigade of Hooker's Center Grand Division across the Rappahannock above Fredericksburg at Kelly's Ford while crossing his main infantry force near the Seddon House six miles below. On December 26, orders were issued to portions of Hooker's men to prepare to cover Averell's intended crossing. Lee, like Burnside, did not remain idle. Stuart led a raid of 1,800 cavalry troopers on the day after Christmas from Kelly's Ford northwest to Dumfries, Fairfax Courthouse, Warrenton and Culpeper and returning to Fredericksburg six days later. The Dumfries Raid captured twenty-five Federal supply wagons along with at least two hundred prisoners, further embarrassing the Army of the Potomac.[227]

Burnside's efforts were further embarrassed before they could begin by his own subordinates. Franklin and Smith wrote directly to Lincoln offering their views on the future operations of the Army of the Potomac and recommending another operation on the peninsula between the York and James Rivers similar to McClellan's Peninsula Campaign earlier that spring. The new offensive they proposed required the transfer of troops from Fredericksburg to the James River. Lincoln thanked them for their advice but made it clear that any transfer of troops to the James would still require a significant force at Fredericksburg to protect Washington. Franklin and Smith did not seem to understand that in his reply to them Lincoln had mildly rebuked them for bypassing the normal chain of command for speaking directly to him about military strategy without first consulting Burnside. Intentional or not, Burnside's leadership was being undermined.

The two senior generals of the Left Grand Division did not give up in their efforts to express their concerns about Burnside and the Army of the Potomac. Franklin granted leave requests for VI Corps division commander Brigadier General John Newton and one of his brigade commanders, Brigadier General John C. Cochrane, to travel to Washington on December 30. Cochrane had been a member of the U.S. House of Representatives from New York, while Newton's father had represented a Virginia district in the same body for more than thirty years. Despite their claim that their intentions to see Lincoln was by happenstance, Newton and Cochrane sought prominent individuals of influence and authority to express their views on the state of the army. They recounted to members of the Joint Committee on the Conduct of the War their conversation with Lincoln that many of the officers and soldiers in the Army of the Potomac had become dispirited in the aftermath of Fredericksburg and did not expect success in another offensive across the Rappahannock. It was quite clear to Lincoln that there seemed to be some dissension in the Army of the Potomac, and he ordered Burnside to halt his planned operation. "I have good reason for saying that you must not make a general movement without letting me know of it," Lincoln stated.[228]

Traveling to Washington on New Year's Day (after the president had signed the Emancipation Proclamation), Burnside met with Lincoln for frank discussion of his strategy. Burnside wanted permission to proceed with his offensive. Lincoln denied his request. Informed that some of his general officers had visited Washington expressing a lack of confidence in his new plans, Burnside called for their dismissal. Not making headway with his superior, Burnside offered his resignation and suggested Halleck and Secretary Stanton do the same since the general public was also aimed at them for Fredericksburg. Lincoln suggested an adjournment of their meeting to reconvene later that day. When Burnside returned, Lincoln was joined by Halleck and Stanton. Burnside reiterated his offer to resign as well as his suggestion that Halleck and Stanton do the same. He also appealed to Lincoln for the identity of the two generals who had visited the president (although he might have already suspected they were Newton and Cochrane) and the approval of their dismissal from the army. He received nothing when he returned to the army at Falmouth on January 2, 1863.[229]

By January 15, Burnside had hashed out a new offensive that Lincoln and Halleck felt was ready to be put into place. His new plan was to cross the Rappahannock, with Franklin's and Hooker's commands at both U.S. and Banks Fords, respectively, above Fredericksburg. Sumner would follow the next day after making demonstrations in the face of Lee's army. A two-corps Reserve Grand Division under Major General Franz Sigel would march to Falmouth from Stafford Courthouse to fill the gaps between Sumner and the maneuvering units heading upriver. The movement commenced on January 20, and all seemed promising. By the following day, continuous downpours halted further movement of the Army of the Potomac. Burnside hoped that the river crossing could commence by the early morning of the twenty-second. The torrential rain turned the roads into instant mud. Exhausted troops and horses, coupled with wagons and artillery trains, stuck in the mire and muck, halting further operations. In response, Lee ordered two of Longstreet's divisions (Richard Anderson's and Pickett's) west along the Orange Turnpike, where their men entrenched themselves to cover enemy crossings at Banks and U.S. Fords. Morale had already sapped the strength of the Army of the Potomac. Burnside ordered a withdrawal of his army back to its original camp on January 23, ending Burnside's "Mud March."[230]

Stifled by his superiors in Washington and mistrusting the subordinates in his command, Burnside composed a set of general orders in which he dismissed nine officers from the Army of the Potomac "subject to the approval of the President of the United States." Heading the list of dismissed officers was Joseph Hooker, who never held Burnside's trust and confidence. Accused of "unjust and unnecessary criticisms of the actions of his superior officers," Hooker was seen as an individual who calculated false impressions of others. He was "a man unfit to hold an important commission during a crisis like the present," Burnside concluded. John Newton was dismissed for visiting Lincoln for the purpose of criticizing Burnside's plans. William Franklin and William "Baldy" Smith were included in a list of officers whom Burnside deemed to "be of no further service to this army." Upon the suggestion of his military aides, Burnside sought a meeting with Lincoln for his approval of "General Orders No. 8."

Burnside met with Lincoln in Washington, showing him the orders. Burnside took the further step to resign if Lincoln did not approve it. Lincoln would not assent to its publication until he consulted with his "advisers." Burnside replied that if that was the case, Lincoln would not approve it. Lincoln asked Burnside to return the next day. On January 25, 1863, Lincoln relieved Burnside "at his own request" from command. Sumner was relieved from duty with the Army of the Potomac, also "at his own request," along with Franklin, who was simply relieved from duty. "Fighting Joe" Hooker was appointed to command the Army of the Potomac.[231]

Burnside had been in command of the Army of the Potomac for two months, two weeks and two days. In his farewell order, he expressed his gratitude to the soldiers for their "courage, patience, and endurance that under more favorable circumstances would have accomplished great results." Encouraging them to continue these virtues, Burnside commended them to Hooker, who he diplomatically described as "the brave and skillful general who has so long been identified with your organization, and who is now to command you, your full and cordial support and co-operation, and you will deserve success." This advice was not only intended for the soldiers but also for their new commander.[232]

Conclusion

A Mighty Large Elephant

A few days before Lincoln's Emancipation Proclamation freeing slaves in the rebellious states took effect on January 1, 1863, Robert E. Lee filed a deed in Richmond emancipating his deceased father-in-law's slaves as stipulated in his will. As one of the executors, Lee had five years from the death of George Washington Parke Custis to fulfill this obligation. This action may have been a moot point since the Custis-Lee House at Arlington had been under Federal occupation since the start of the war. For him, slavery was not the issue at stake in the present war. In Lee's estimation, preserving the rights in the states without usurpation by federal authorities caused the formation of the Confederacy and the Emancipation Proclamation to be a groundless document.

The Battle of Fredericksburg ended a year of success for the Confederate commander with one of the easiest victories that he and his men would ever experience in the war. To Lee's regret, he was forced to make a defensive stand in an area that geographically held very little opportunities for counteroffensive moments that could destroy the Federal Army of the Potomac. "The war is not yet ended," he reminded the troops in his congratulatory order two days after his emancipation of the Arlington slaves. "The enemy is still numerous and strong, and the country demands of the army a renewal of its heroic efforts in her behalf. Nobly has it responded to her call in the past, and she will never appeal in vain to its courage and patriotism." Lee invoked continued divine guidance to "insure the safety, peace, and happiness of our beloved country, and add new luster to the already imperishable name of the Army of Northern Virginia."[233]

Lincoln had revealed his own thoughts to the officers and men of the Army of the Potomac on December 22, 1862:

> *I have just read your commanding general's report of the battle of Fredericksburg. Although you were not successful, the attempt was not an error, nor the failure other than accident. The courage with which you, in an open field maintained the contest against an intrenched foe, and the consummate skill and success with which you crossed and recrossed the river, in the face of the enemy, show that you possess all the qualities of a great army, which will yet give victory to the cause of the country and of popular government.*[234]

Lincoln's assessment of the Battle of Fredericksburg can be taken at face value. The defeat was not an "error" but an unfortunate "accident." It was an accident in Lincoln's mind as he sought to achieve his broader goals for the Union war effort, which now clearly included emancipation. Fredericksburg, until recent years, has earned the reputation of being one of many battles lost by the Army of the Potomac in the eastern theatre. Recent scholars have now alluded to the fact that Lincoln's change of commanders and strategy during the second half of 1862 in defeating Robert E. Lee and the Army of Northern Virginia in a clear and decisive battle was in part to secure military enforcement of his initial gradual and compensated emancipation policies. Fredericksburg was not simply the last major battle fought that year, starting with the end of the Peninsula Campaign continuing through Second Bull Run and Antietam; it was the battle that Lincoln hoped would achieve the desired military success to sustain emancipation as part of the Union war effort. Lincoln, as commander in chief, viewed his powers and responsibilities in the broadest of terms, with the military being a necessary but still subordinate component in achieving his goals. In the larger view of the president, Fredericksburg was an "accident," although many Federal soldiers did not share the same view at the end of 1862 and in the first weeks of 1863.

The Emancipation Proclamation, formally issued on January 1, 1863, freed slaves in the states under rebellion exempting the slave border states and specific areas under Federal occupation. Conspicuously absent were any references to compensated emancipation or colonization of freed slaves that had been a part of his Preliminary Emancipation Proclamation. What was new in the final document was the official sanction of enlisting African Americans into the U.S. Army and Navy. Frederick Douglass in an editorial encouraged Lincoln not to "trifle with the wounds of his bleeding country… while the cold earth around Fredericksburg is wet with warm blood of our patriot soldiers—every one of whom was slain by slaveholding rebels." A *Richmond Daily Dispatch* editorial responded in kind to the sentiments Douglass expressed: "The South has given its answer to Lincoln's proclamation of emancipation at Fredericksburg and Murfreesboro."[235]

"This war will never be terminated until one side or the other has been well whipped," wrote George Meade at the time of Hooker's replacement of Burnside, "and this result cannot be brought about except by fighting." Lincoln had earlier echoed Meade's sentiments when he remarked on McClellan's apparent lack of striking a decisive blow against Lee. Speaking to volunteers of the Western Sanitary Commission, Lincoln said, "They have gotten into their heads that we are going to get out of this fix, somehow by strategy! General McClellan thinks he is going to whip the rebels by strategy; and the army has got the same notion. They have no idea that the war is to be carried on and put through by hard, tough fighting…and no headway is going to be made while this delusion lasts."[236]

Joseph Hooker was the new man to lead the Army of the Potomac to victory in spite of Lincoln's reservations that he had been one of several officers who had undermined his superior, Ambrose Burnside, as well as had a loose tongue among Washington circles in his criticism of the present administration. It was Hooker's ambition that Lincoln hoped to capitalize on in his quest to enforce and sustain his military and war policies. "What I now ask of you is military success, and I will risk the dictatorship," the president wrote Hooker. Daniel G. Crotty, of the Third Michigan Infantry, probably expressed the general sentiments of the army on Hooker:

Now, we all feel that General Hooker will be like the poor man that won the elephant at the raffle. After he got the animal he did not know what to do with him. So with fighting Joseph. He is now in command of a mighty large elephant, and it will remain to be seen if he knows what to do with him. All know that General Hooker can command and fight a division to perfection, but to take a great army like ours in hand, and cope with the great rebel chief successfully, is another thing. But we will wait and see, and like good soldiers, obey orders and go where we are sent, even unto death.[237]

Notes

INTRODUCTION

1. Jane Howison Beale, *The Journal of Jane Howison Beale, Fredericksburg, Virginia, 1850–1862* (Fredericksburg, VA: Historic Fredericksburg Foundation, Inc., 1995), 62; John Hampden Chamberlayne, *Ham Chamberlayne—Virginian: Letters and Papers of an Artillery Officer in the War for Southern Independence, 1861–1865* (Richmond, VA: Dietz Press, 1932), 62; Noel G. Harrison, *Fredericksburg Civil War Sites, April 1861–November 1862*, vol. 1 (Lynchburg, VA: H.E. Howard, Inc., 1995), 16–17; U.S. War Department, *War of the Rebellion: A Compilation of the Official Records of the Union and Confederate Armies*, ser. I, vol. 12, pt. 1 (Washington, D.C.: Government Printing Office, 1880–1901), 427–28, and pt. 3, 43 (hereafter cited as *OR*).
2. Francis Winthrop Palfrey, *The Antietam and Fredericksburg*, vol. 5, *Campaigns of the Civil War* (New York: Charles Scribner's Sons, 1882), 190.
3. Articles on Fredericksburg in the *Battles and Leaders* series include those written by Federal generals such as Darius N. Couch and William F. Smith, as well as those from Confederate generals James Longstreet, Lafayette McLaws, Robert Ransom and Joseph B. Kershaw. See Robert Underwood Johnson and Clarence Clough Buel, eds., *Battles and Leaders of the Civil War*, vol. 3 (New York: Century Company, 1884, 1888), 70–147.

4. Edward J. Stackpole, *Drama on the Rappahannock: The Fredericksburg Campaign* (New York: Bonanza Books, 1957), xvii. Other works dealing with the Fredericksburg Campaign written by military professionals include British army officers George F.R. Henderson, *The Campaign of Fredericksburg: November–December 1862, A Tactical Study for Officers of Volunteers* (London, UK: Kegan Paul, Trench, and Company, 1886) and G.W. Redway, *Fredericksburg: A Study in War* (New York: MacMillan Company, 1906), as well as U.S. Army officer Vorin E. Whan Jr., *Fiasco at Fredericksburg* (State College: Pennsylvania State University Press, 1961; reprint, Gaithersburg, MD: Olde Soldiers Books, Inc.).

5. It should be noted that numerous monographs, book chapters and articles on particular aspects of Fredericksburg within the last sixteen years have anticipated and in several respects paved the way for Rable's and O'Reilly's more recent publications. These include Frank A. O'Reilly, *"Stonewall" Jackson at Fredericksburg: The Battle of Prospect Hill, December 13, 1862* (Lynchburg, VA: H.E. Howard Inc., 1993); Harrison, *Fredericksburg Civil War Sites, April 1861–November 1862*, vol. 1; Noel G. Harrison, *Fredericksburg Civil War Sites, December 1862–April 1865*, vol. 2 (Lynchburg, VA: H.E. Howard Inc., 1995); Gary W. Gallagher, ed., *The Fredericksburg Campaign: Decision on the Rappahannock* (Chapel Hill: University of North Carolina Press, 1995); Theodore P. Savas and David A. Woodbury, eds., *Blood on the Rappahannock: The Battle of Fredericksburg—Essays on Union and Confederate Leadership*, vol. 4, no. 4, *Civil War Regiments* (Eldorado Hills, CA: Regimental Studies Inc., 1995); and Frank A. O'Reilly, "Battle of Fredericksburg: Lee's Incomplete Victory," *America's Civil War* (November 2001), 30–37.

6. George C. Rable, *Fredericksburg! Fredericksburg!* (Chapel Hill: University of North Carolina Press, 2002), 2–5, 432; Francis Augustin O'Reilly, *The Fredericksburg Campaign: Winter War on the Rappahannock* (Baton Rouge: Louisiana State University Press, 2003, 2006), 5–6, 495, 498–99.

7. Carl von Clausewitz, *On War*, ed. Anatol Rapoport (1832; New York: Penguin Books, 1982), 402; Rable, *Fredericksburg! Fredericksburg!*, 432.

8. Beale, *Journal*, 73; John M. Washington, "Memorys of the Past" in David W. Blight, *A Slave No More: Two Men Who Escaped to Freedom Including Their Own Narratives of Emancipation* (New York: Mariner Books, 2009), 189–90.

CHAPTER 1

9. Don E. Fehrenbacher, ed. "To Albert G. Hodges, April 4, 1864," *Abraham Lincoln: Speeches and Writings, 1859–1865* (New York: Library of America, 1989), 586.

10. *OR*, ser. I, vol. 3, 466–67, 469; *OR*, ser. III, vol. 2, 42–43.

11. *OR*, ser. I, vol. 2, 53, 649–50; John B. Cary to Benjamin F. Butler, March 9, 1891, in Jessie Marshall Ames, ed. *Private and Official Correspondence of General Benjamin F. Butler During the Civil War*, vol. 1 (Norwood, MA: Plimpton Press, 1917), 102–3; Butler, *Butler's Book: A Review of His Legal, Political, and Military Career* (Boston: A.M. Thayer, 1892), 256–58; Edward L. Pierce, "The Contrabands at Fortress Monroe," *Atlantic Monthly* 49 (November 1861), 627–28; Robert F. Engs, *Freedom's First Generation: Black Hampton, Virginia, 1861–1890* (Philadelphia: University of Pennsylvania Press, 1979), 20; U.S. Congress, "An Act to Confiscate Property for Insurrectionary Purposes, August 6, 1861" in George P. Sanger, ed., *Statutes at Large, Treaties, and Proclamations, of the United States of America*, vol. 12 (Boston: Little, Brown and Company, 186), 319.

12. *OR*, ser. III, vol. 2, 276, 282.

13. Stephen B. Oates, *With Malice Toward None: A Life of Abraham Lincoln* (1977; New York: Harper Perennial, 1994), 182–83. For a book-length examination of the Joint Committee on the Conduct of the War see Bruce Tap, *Over Lincoln's Shoulder* (Lawrence: University Press of Kansas, 1998).

14. David Herbert Donald, *Lincoln* (New York: Simon and Schuster, 1995), 331; "Message to Congress, April 16, 1862," *Abraham Lincoln: Speeches and Writings*, 316.

15. "Draft for Compensated Emancipation in Delaware, ca. November 1861" in *Abraham Lincoln: Speeches and Writings*, 276–78; Allen C. Guelzo, *Lincoln's Emancipation Proclamation* (New York: Simon and Schuster, 2004), 57–58; "Annual Message to Congress, December 3, 1861," *Abraham Lincoln: Speeches and Writings*, 291–92; "Message to Congress, March 6, 1862," *Abraham Lincoln: Speeches and Writings*, 307–8; "To James A. McDougall, March 14, 1862," *Abraham Lincoln: Speeches and Writings*, 310; "To Horace Greeley, March 24, 1862," *Abraham Lincoln: Speeches and Writings*, 312; Donald, *Lincoln*, 348.

16. "Appeal to Border-State Representatives for Compensated Emancipation, Washington, D.C., July 12, 1862," *Abraham Lincoln: Speeches and Writings*, 340; Guelzo, *Lincoln's Emancipation Proclamation*, 108–9.

17. "Address on Colonization to a Committee of Colored Men, Washington, D.C., August 14, 1862," *Abraham Lincoln: Speeches and Writings*, 353–57; Donald, *Lincoln*, 367; Guelzo, *Lincoln's Emancipation Proclamation*, 142–44; Doris Kearns Goodwin, *Team of Rivals: The Political Genius of Abraham Lincoln* (New York: Simon and Schuster, 2006), 469; "The President and His Speeches," *Douglass' Monthly* (September 1862) in Philip S. Foner, ed., *Frederick Douglass: Selected Speeches and Writings* (Chicago, IL: Lawrence Hill Books, 1999), 512.

18. "Reply to Chicago Emancipation Memorial, Washington, D.C., September 13, 1862," *Abraham Lincoln: Speeches and Writings*, 361–67; Oates, *With Malice Toward None*, 317.

19. Donald, *Lincoln*, 367–68; Guelzo, *Lincoln's Emancipation Proclamation*, 144; Goodwin, *Team of Rivals*, 470; "To Horace Greely, August 22, 1862," *Abraham Lincoln: Speeches and Writings*, 358.

20. "To Reverdy Johnson, July 26, 1862," *Abraham Lincoln: Speeches and Writings*, 344.

21. George B. McClellan, *The Civil War Papers of George B. McClellan: Selected Correspondence, 1860–1865*, ed. Stephen W. Sears (New York: Da Capo Press, 1992), 345–46; Stephen W. Sears, *George B. McClellan: The Young Napoleon* (New York: Ticknor and Fields, 1988), 227–29; Stephen W. Sears, *To the Gates of Richmond: The Peninsula Campaign* (1992; New York: Mariner Books, 2001), 350–51; Goodwin, *Team of Rivals*, 451.

22. Gideon Welles, *Diary of Gideon Welles: Secretary of the Navy Under Lincoln and Johnson*, vol. 1, *1861–March 30, 1864* (Boston: Houghton Mifflin Company, 1911), 70; Donald, *Lincoln*, 363–64.

23. *OR*, ser. III, vol. 2, 584–85; Oates, *With Malice Toward None*, 310–11; Donald, *Lincoln*, 365–66; Mark E. Neely, *The Last Best Hope on Earth: Abraham Lincoln and the Promise of America* (Cambridge, MA: Harvard University Press, 1993), 108–10; Goodwin, *Team of Rivals*, 464–68.

24. "Preliminary Emancipation Proclamation, September 22, 1862," *Abraham Lincoln: Speeches and Writings*, 368–70. Hennessy and Goodwin have asserted that Federal military efforts for sustaining Lincoln's preliminary emancipation proclamation began with Pope and his Army of Virginia. Guelzo has argued that Pope's expected campaign in Virginia was among several events causing Lincoln to hope that emancipation was forthcoming. See John J. Hennessy, *Return to Bull Run: The Campaign and Battle of Second Manassas* (New York: Simon and Schuster, 1993), 17; Goodwin, *Team of Rivals*, 473; and Guelzo, *Lincoln's Emancipation Proclamation*, 144, 154–56.

25. *OR*, ser. I, vol. 19, pt. 2, 644; J.B. Jones, *A Rebel War Clerk's Diary at the Confederate States Capital*, vol. 1 (Philadelphia, PA: J.B. Lippincott and Company, 1866), 157, 164; O'Reilly, *Fredericksburg Campaign*, 10.

26. Goodwin, *Team of Rivals*, 484; Michael P. Johnson, ed., *Abraham Lincoln, Slavery, and the Civil War: Selected Writings and Speeches* (New York: Bedford/St. Martin's, 2001), 174.

27. "To George B. McClellan, October 24/25, 1862," *Abraham Lincoln: Speeches and Writings*, 379–80. For accounts of McClellan's transfer of command of the Army of the Potomac to Burnside, see Sears, *Landscape Turned Red*, 339–41; Sears, *George B. McClellan*, 340–41; William Marvel, *Burnside* (Chapel Hill: University of North Carolina Press, 1991), 159–60; Rable, *Fredericksburg! Fredericksburg!*, 42–44; and O'Reilly, *Fredericksburg Campaign*, 1–3.

28. Welles, *Diary*, vol. 1, 182; "Charles Francis Adams, Jr., to Henry Adams, November 19, 1862," in Worthington Chauncey Ford, ed., *A Cycle of Adams Letters*, vol. 1 (Boston: Houghton Mifflin Company, 1920), 194.

29. Francis Adams Donaldson, *Inside the Army of the Potomac: The Civil War Experience of Captain Francis Adams Donaldson*, ed. J. Gregory Acken (Mechanicsburg, PA: Stackpole Books, 1998), 161–62; C.W. Bardeen, *A Little Fifer's War Diary* (Syracuse, NY, 1910), 83; George Gordon Meade, *Life and Letters of George Gordon Meade, Major-General United States Army*, vol. 1 (New York: Charles Scribner's Sons, 1913), 325. One of the more glaring suggestions that the Army of the Potomac did not vigorously pursue Lee's army after Antietam (Sharpsburg) because of Lincoln's policies, especially the Preliminary Emancipation, stemmed from statements of Major John J. Key, of Halleck's staff, who had a brother on McClellan's staff. In what seemed to be an innocent discussion speculating on why McClellan did not defeat the Confederates, Major Key replied, "That is not the game. The object is that neither army shall get much advantage of the other; that both shall be kept in the field till they are exhausted, when we will make a compromise and save slavery." Summoned to the White House in late September, Key explained himself to Lincoln on his reported statements, which he acknowledged. His loyalty to the Union was endorsed by witnesses present at this meeting. Seeking to make an example of Key and serving notice to McClellan about who held supreme authority over the war effort, Lincoln dismissed Key from the service. "In my view," Lincoln concluded, "it is wholly inadmissable for any gentleman holding a military commission from the United States to utter such sentiments." McClellan soon issued orders to the army that the military

served to sustain the policies of civil authorities. James Mcpherson has recently noted that McClellan, in that order, could not resist what Lincoln could have interpreted as a veiled threat when he wrote, "The remedy for political errors, if any are committed, is to be found only in the action of the people at the polls." McClellan became the Democratic nominee for president against Lincoln in 1864. See "Record of Dismissal of John J. Key, September 26–27, 1862," *Abraham Lincoln: Speeches and Writings*, 373–74; *OR*, ser. I, vol. 19, pt. 2, 395–96; Sears, *Landscape Turned Red*, 319–22; Sears, *George B. McClellan*, 326–27; James M. McPherson, *Tried By War: Abraham Lincoln as Commander in Chief* (New York: Penguin Press, 2008), 134.

30. For an excellent treatment of the Federal military campaigns in Kentucky and Tennessee in the fall of 1862 as they relate to Burnside in Virginia, see Peter Cozzens, *No Better Place To Die: The Battle of Stones River* (Urbana: University of Illinois Press), 12–28, and also O'Reilly, *"Stonewall" Jackson at Fredericksburg*, 6.

31. "Annual Message to Congress, December 1, 1862," *Abraham Lincoln: Speeches and Writings*, 407, 415.

32. "Emancipation Proclaimed," *Douglass' Monthly* (October 1862) in *Frederick Douglass: Selected Speeches and Writings*, 518.

CHAPTER 2

33. James M. McPherson and James K. Hogue, *Ordeal By Fire: The Civil War and Reconstruction*, 4th ed. (New York: McGraw-Hill, 2009), 187–88; O'Reilly, *Fredericksburg Campaign*, 6.

34. William R. Stilwell, *The Stilwell Letters: A Georgian in Longstreet's Corps, Army of Northern Virginia*, ed. Ronald H. Moseley (Atlanta, GA: Mercer University Press, 2002), 82; Donaldson, *Inside the Army of the Potomac*, 172.

35. Emory M. Thomas, *Robert E. Lee: A Biography* (New York: W.W. Norton and Company, 1995), 64, 269.

36. Robert E. Lee, "Life of General Henry Lee" in Henry Lee, *Memoirs of the War in the Southern Department of the United States*, ed. Robert E. Lee (1824; New York: University Publishing Company, 1869), 51; Thomas, *Robert E. Lee*, 79; Richard B. McCaslin, *Lee in the Shadow of Washington* (Baton Rouge: Louisiana State University Press, 2004), 12.

37. George W. Cullum, *Biographical Register of Officers and Graduates of the U.S. Military Academy at West Point, N.Y.*, vol. 1, *1802–1840*, 3rd ed. (New York:

Houghton Mifflin and Company, 1891), 420–21; Thomas, *Robert E. Lee*, 58, 63, 69, 86–92, 94–97, 99, 101, 110.

38. Scott quoted in Thomas, *Robert E. Lee*, 127; Cullum, *Biographical Register*, vol. 1, 420–21.

39. Cullum, *Biographical Register*, vol. 1, 421; Thomas, *Robert E. Lee*, 152–62.

40. Cullum, *Biographical Register*, vol. 1, 421; Thomas, *Robert E. Lee*, 173–78.

41. Thomas, *Robert E. Lee*, 179–83.

42. Lee quoted in Thomas, *Robert E. Lee*, 173.

43. Cullum, *Biographical Register*, vol. 1, 421; Thomas, *Robert E. Lee*, 183–87.

44. Lee quoted in Thomas, *Robert E. Lee*, 187–88.

45. Ibid., 268.

46. Edward Porter Alexander, *Fighting for the Confederacy: The Personal Recollections of General Edward Porter Alexander*, ed. Gary W. Gallagher (Chapel Hill: University of North Carolina Press, 1998), 91, 166; James L. Morrison Jr., *"The Best School in the World": West Point, the Pre-Civil War Years, 1833–1866* (Kent, OH: Kent State University Press, 1986), 78.

47. Augustus Woodbury, *Ambrose Everett Burnside* (Providence, RI: N. Bangs Williams and Company, 1882), 6–8; Marvel, *Burnside*, 2–5; George W. Cullum, *Biographical Register of the Officer and Graduates of the U.S. Military Academy*, vol. 2, *1841–1867* (New York: D. Van Nostrand, 1868), 191. According to Marvel, Burnside's middle name, "Everts," became "Everett" due to a clerical error on his diploma, and he never changed it. (A similar clerical error at West Point happened to a cadet just graduating when Burnside's class arrived for summer encampment. This cadet in the class of 1843 entered the academy as "Hiram Ulysses Grant," but his mother's maiden name was inadvertently substituted for his middle name, and he became thus "Ulysses Simpson Grant.")

48. Cullum, *Biographical Register*, vol. 2, 184–85, 189, 192–93, 196–97, 200–202, 206; Benjamin Perley Poore, *The Life and Public Services of Ambrose E. Burnside: Soldier, Citizen, Statesman* (Providence, RI: J.A. and R.A. Reid, 1882), 36.

49. Cullum, *Biographical Register*, vol. 2, 191; Woodbury, *Ambrose Everett Burnside*, 8–9; Poore, *Life and Public Services*, 53–54; Marvel, *Burnside*, 5–6.

50. Poore, *Life and Public Services*, 57; Marvel, *Burnside*, 6.

51. Poore, *Life and Public Services*, 60; Marvel, *Burnside*, 9.

52. Marvel, *Burnside*, 9.

53. Cullum, *Biographical Register*, vol. 2, 191; Woodbury, *Ambrose Everett Burnside*, 9–10; Poore, *Life and Public Services*, 64–65; Marvel, *Burnside*, 10.

54. Woodbury, *Ambrose Everett Burnside*, 10–12; Poore, *Life and Public Services*, 67–76; Marvel, *Burnside*, 10–11.

55. Woodbury, *Ambrose Everett Burnside*, 12–13; Poore, *Life and Public Services*, 78, 83–88; Cullum, *Biographical Register*, vol. 2, 206; Marvel, *Burnside*, 12–13.

56. Poore, *Life and Public Services*, 88–89; Marvel, *Burnside*, 14; Sears, *George B. McClellan*, 58.

57. Marvel, *Burnside*, 16–31.

58. Cullum, *Biographical Register*, vol. 2, 191; Poore, *Life and Public Services*, 123–52; Marvel, *Burnside*, 41–96.

59. Sears, *Landscape Turned Red*, 171.

60. *OR*, ser. I, vol. 19, pt. 2, 685–87, 698, 702.

61. Most modern scholarship on the Fredericksburg Campaign has been consistent with Confederate strengths. The *Official Records* list 78,040 "present for duty" on the returns of December 10, 1862, but a maximum of 85,175 for "aggregate present," accounting for those absent for sickness, leave or detached duty. Whan (1961) gives 78,513 for the Confederate strength in a work focusing primarily on the Union Army of the Potomac. Savas in his introductory essay in *Blood on the Rappahannock* (1995) estimates 78,000. Rable in *Fredericksburg! Fredericksburg!* (2002) estimates 80,000, while O'Reilly in *Fredericksburg Campaign* (2003) gives the Confederates 78,000. See *OR*, ser. I, vol. 21, 1,057; Whan, *Fiasco at Fredericksburg*, 2; Theodore P. Savas, "The Battle of Fredericksburg Revisited," in *Blood on the Rappahannock*, iii; Rable, *Fredericksburg! Fredericksburg!*, 148; and O'Reilly, *Fredericksburg Campaign*, 7.

62. *OR*, ser. I, vol. 19, pt. 2, 633–34, 643, 698–99.

63. Cullum, *Biographical Register*, vol. 2, 70–71; James Longstreet, *From Manassas to Appomattox: Memoirs of the Civil War in America* (Philadelphia, PA: J.B. Lippincott and Company, 1896), 17–18; G. Moxley Sorrel, *Recollections of a Confederate Staff Officer* (New York: Neale Publishing Company, 1905), 103; Jeffrey D. Wert, *General James Longstreet: The Confederacy's Most Controversial General* (New York: Touchstone, 1993), 26–32, 34.

64. Cullum, *Biographical Register*, vol. 2, 70; Wert, *General James Longstreet*, 38–45.

65. Wert, *General James Longstreet*, 46–50.

66. Sorrel, *Recollections of a Confederate Staff Officer*, 116.

67. James I. Robertson Jr., *Stonewall Jackson: The Man, the Soldier, the Legend* (New York: MacMillan Publishing, 1997), 27, 40; John G. Waugh, *Class of 1846—From West Point to Appomattox: Stonewall Jackson, George McClellan and Their Brothers* (New York: Ballantine Books, 1994), xiv–xvi.

68. Robertson, *Stonewall Jackson*, 33–44; Waugh, *Class of 1846*, 21, 55.

69. Robertson, *Stonewall Jackson*, 47–78.

70. Robertson, *Stonewall Jackson*, 107–219.

71. Robertson, *Stonewall Jackson*, 263–64, 835 (n. 37).

72. Cullum, *Biographical Register*, vol. 2, 375; Emory M. Thomas, *Bold Dragoon: The Life of J.E.B. Stuart* (New York: Harper and Row, 1986), 42; Jeffry D. Wert, *Cavalryman of the Lost Cause: A Biography of J.E.B. Stuart* (New York: Simon and Schuster, 2008), 36–37, 76; Robertson, *Stonewall Jackson*, 235–36.

73. Sears, *To the Gates of Richmond*, 167–73; Thomas, *Bold Dragoon*, 113–29, 158, 173–79; Sears, *Landscape Turned Red*, 327–28; and Wert, *Cavalryman of the Lost Cause*, 94–103, 168–76.

74. Modern scholarship on Federal strength during the Fredericksburg Campaign has some variance. The *Official Records* list 122,024 "Present for Duty" instead of "Aggregate Present" on the returns of December 10, 1862, for the units actually involved in movements and actions leading up to the December 13 battle. Stackpole (1957) bases the minimum Federal strength of 114,873 on the *Papers of the Military Historical Society of Massachusetts* numbers compiled by former Confederate officer William Allan. Stackpole's maximum number of Federal strength is based on the *Official Records* at 122,009. Whan (1961) takes his Federal strength of 120,821 from Captain Thomas Livermore's *Numbers and Losses in the Civil War* and the strength of the army when McClellan turned over command to Burnside. Savas in his introductory essay in *Blood on the Rappahannock* (1995) estimates a strength of 115,000. Rable (2002) estimates 120,000. O'Reilly (2003) presents the Federal strength at 135,000, but it is not clear if this number include the forces making up the "Reserve Grand Division" under Major General Franz Sigel. See *OR*, ser. I, vol. 21, 1,121; Stackpole, *Drama on the Rappahannock*, 276–77; Whan, *Fiasco at Fredericksburg*, 1; Savas, "The Battle of Fredericksburg Revisited," in *Blood on the Rappahannock*, iii; Rable, *Fredericksburg! Fredericksburg!*, 144; and O'Reilly, *Fredericksburg Campaign*, 7.

75. Sears, *Landscape Turned Red*, 216.

76. Francis B. Heitman, *Historical Register of the United States Army* (Washington, D.C.: Government Printing Office, 1890), 625; Robert S. Lanier, ed., *The Photographic History of the Civil War*, vol. 10, *Armies and Leaders* (New York: Review of Reviews, 1911), 188, 190; Moorefield Storey, *Charles Sumner: American Statesman* (Boston: Hougton Mifflin Company, 1900), 2; Edward L. Pierce, *Memoirs and Letters of Charles Sumner*, vol. 1, *1811–1838* (Boston: Roberts Brothers, 1893), 26.

77. Heitman, *Historical Register of the United States Army*, 625; C.B. Galbreath, "John Brown," *Ohio Archeological and Historical Quarterly* 30 (1921), 239; Stephen B. Oates, *To Purge This Land with Blood: A Biography of John Brown*, 2nd ed. (Amherst: University of Massachusetts Press, 1984), 155–61; Thomas, *Bold Dragoon*, 46.

78. Donald, *Lincoln*, 273, 278, 340–41; Sears, *To the Gates of Richmond*, 8, 71; Heitman, *Historical Register of the United States Army*, 625.

79. Mark A. Snell, *From First to Last: The Life of Major William B. Franklin* (New York: Fordham University Press, 2002), 2–10.

80. Cullum, *Biographical Register*, vol. 2, 72.

81. Cullum, *Biographical Register*, vol. 2, 72–73; O'Reilly, *Fredericksburg Campaign*, 24.

82. Hennessy, *Return to Bull Run*, 465, 468.

83. Snell, *From First to Last*, 203.

84. Samuel P. Bates, "Hooker's Comments on Chancellorsville," in *Battles and Leaders of the Civil War*, vol. 3, 217.

85. Walter H. Hebert, *Fighting Joe Hooker* (New York: Bobbs-Merrill, 1944; Lincoln: University of Nebraska Press, 1999), 17, 20.

86. J.C. Featherston, "Gen. Jubal Anderson Early," *Confederate Veteran* 26 (October 1918): 430; Millard Kessler Bushong, *Old Jube: A Biography of General Jubal A. Early* (Boyce, VA: Carr Publishing Company, 1955), 12–13; Charles C. Osborne, *Jubal: The Life and Times of Jubal A. Early, CSA, Defender of the Lost Cause* (Baton Rouge: Louisiana State University Press, 1992), 14; Hebert, *Fighting Joe Hooker*, 21; Cullum, *Biographical Register*, vol. 1, 521–22, 529, 531–33, 536–38, 546–47.

87. Cullum, *Biographical Register*, vol. 1, 536–37; and Hebert, *Fighting Joe Hooker*, 23–24.

88. Hebert, *Fighting Joe Hooker*, 28–35.

89. Francis B. Heitman, *Historical Register and Dictionary of the United States Army*, vol. 1 (Washington, D.C.: Government Printing Office, 1903), 540; Hebert, *Fighting Joe Hooker*, 38–48.

90. Hebert, *Fighting Joe Hooker*, 49.

91. "To George B. McClellan, October 13, 1862," *Abraham Lincoln: Speeches and Writings*, 376–78; *OR*, ser. I, vol. 19, pt. 2, 552–53.

92. U.S. Congress, *Report of the Joint Committee on the Conduct of the War*, pt. 1, *Army of the Potomac* (Washington, D.C.: Government Printing Office, 1863), 649 (hereafter referred to as *JCCW*). Also see *OR*, ser. I, vol. 21, pt. 2, 148–49, for a memorandum prepared for Burnside outlining the orders issued while McClellan was still in command for pontoon bridges

in Maryland to be transferred to Washington, D.C. Some current scholarship suggests that McClellan had contemplated shifting the Army of the Potomac to the Fredericksburg line once he crossed the Rapidan River and that Burnside simply adhered to his plan instead of originating it himself. See Sears, *George B. McClellan*, 337; Marvel, *Burnside*, 164; and O'Reilly, *Fredericksburg Campaign*, 20.

93. *JCCW*, pt. 1, 682; Marvel, *Burnside*, 164–65; *OR*, ser. I, vol. 19, pt. 2, 579, 581–82.

94. For a narrative of Burnside's opening operations on November 15, see O'Reilly, *Fredericksburg Campaign*, 25–27.

95. *OR*, ser. I, vol. 21, 1,014–15; O'Reilly, *Fredericksburg Campaign*, 28, 30.

96. *JCCW*, pt. 1, 657, 658; O'Reilly, *Fredericksburg Campaign*, 30–33.

97. *OR*, ser. I, vol. 21, 1,021; Alan T. Nolan, "Confederate Leadership at Fredericksburg," in *Fredericksburg Campaign: Decision on the Rappahannock*, 30.

98. *OR*, ser. I, vol. 21, 1,021; O'Reilly, *Fredericksburg Campaign*, 34–35.

CHAPTER 3

99. [Varina Howell Davis], *Jefferson Davis, Ex-President of the Confederate States of America: A Memoir*, vol. 2 (New York: Belford Company, 1890), 192–97; Redway, *Fredericksburg*, 72.

100. *OR*, ser. I, vol. 5, 1,103.

101. *OR*, ser. I, vol. 5, 1,100–1,105, and vol. 12, pt. 1, 428.

102. *OR*, ser. I, vol. 21, 549; O'Reilly, *Fredericksburg Campaign*, 35.

103. Matilda Hamilton, "An Eye Witness Account of the Battle of Fredericksburg, December 11–15, 1862," page 6 in Bound Volume #133, Fredericksburg and Spotsylvania National Military Park, National Park Service, Fredericksburg, Virginia.

104. Oscar H. Darter, *Colonial Fredericksburg and Neighborhood in Perspective* (New York: Twayne Publishers, 1957), 46, 48–49, 206–15; Barbara Pratt Willis and Paula S. Felder, *Handbook of Historic Fredericksburg, Virginia* (Fredericksburg, VA: Historic Fredericksburg Foundation, Inc., 1993), 1–4.

105. Harrison, *Fredericksburg Civil War Sites, April 1861–November 1862*, vol. 1, 2–5, 8–10.

106. Spotsylvania County (not including Fredericksburg) had a population of 4,407 (39.9 percent) whites, 6,495 (58.8 percent) slaves and 152 (1.3 percent) free blacks in 1860. Stafford County's population consisted of 4,922 (57.6 percent) whites, 3,314 (38.7 percent) slaves and 319 free

blacks in 1860. Fredericksburg had 3,309 (65.9 percent) whites, 1,291 (25.7 percent) slaves and 422 (8.4 percent) free blacks in 1860. From U.S. Department of the Interior, Office of the Census, *Population of the United States in 1860; Compiled from the Original Returns of the Eighth Census, under the Direction of the Secretary of the Interior*, vol. 1, *Population* (Washington, D.C.: Government Printing Office, 1864; reprint, New York: Norman Ross, 1990), 516–18. For an analytical compilation of the inhabitants of Spotsylvania, Stafford and the city of Fredericksburg using the Eighth (1860) and Ninth (1870) Census, see Cynthia L. Musselman, "The Economic Impact of the Civil War on the City of Fredericksburg, Spotsylvania County, and Stafford County," 2 parts, Bound Manuscript 1984, Fredericksburg and Spotsylvania National Military Park, National Park Service, Fredericksburg, Virginia.

107. Ervin L. Jordan Jr., *Black Confederates and Afro-Yankees in Civil War Virginia* (Charlottesville: University Press of Virginia, 1995), 15, 213; *Fredericksburg (VA) News*, May 7, 1861; Ruth Coder Fitzgerald, *A Different Story: A Black History of Fredericksburg, Stafford, and Spotsylvania* (Fredericksburg, VA: Unicorn Press, 1979), 89–90.

108. Alpheus S. Williams, *From the Cannon's Mouth: The Civil War Letters of Alpheus S. Williams*, ed. Milo M. Quiafe (Lincoln: University of Nebraska Press, 1995), 73; Rufus R. Dawes, *Service with the Sixth Wisconsin* (Marietta, OH: E.R. Alderman and Sons, 1890), 41.

109. Harrison, *Fredericksburg Civil War Sites, April 1861–November 1862*, vol. 1, 120–21, 126–27; Washington, "Memorys of the Past" in Blight, *A Slave No More*, 187–95, 198; Homer D. Musselman, *Stafford County in the Civil War* (Lynchburg, VA: H.E. Howard, Inc., 1995), 88–89.

110. *OR*, ser. I, vol. 21, 783–85, 1,026; Rable, *Fredericksburg! Fredericksburg!*, 83; O'Reilly, *Fredericksburg Campaign*, 35–36.

111. Jones, *A Rebel War Clerk's Diary*, vol. 1, 195–96; Longstreet, *From Manassas to Appomattox*, 296; Rable, *Fredericksburg! Fredericksburg!*, 80–81.

112. Jones, *A Rebel War Clerk's Diary*, vol. 1, 192–95; Rable, *Fredericksburg! Fredericksburg!*, 83; Stilwell, *Stilwell Letters*, 82; O'Reilly, *Fredericksburg Campaign*, 39.

113. O'Reilly, *Fredericksburg Campaign*, 42–43.

114. Rable, *Fredericksburg! Fredericksburg!*, 87–88; O'Reilly, *Fredericksburg Campaign*, 44–48; Josiah F. Murphey, "Reminiscences," page 23 (typescript courtesy of the Boston Public Library) in Bound Volume #248, Fredericksburg and Spotsylvania National Military Park, National Park Service, Fredericksburg, Virginia.

115. Charles F. Walcott, *History of the Twenty-First Regiment Massachusetts Volunteers in the War for the Preservation of the Union, 1861–1865* (Boston: Houghton, Mifflin, and Company, 1882), 230; James Dinkins, *1861 to 1865, by an Old Johnnie: Personal Recollections and Experiences in the Confederate Army* (Cincinnati, OH: Robert Clarke Company, 1897), 66. Also see Oliver Christian Bosbyshell, *The 48th in the War* (Philadelphia, PA: Avil Printing Company, 1895), 93, for an additional Federal account of picket fraternization before the battle.

116. William P. Hopkins, *Seventh Regiment Rhode Island Volunteers in the Civil War, 1862–1865* (Providence, RI: Providence Press, 1903), 34.

117. James Wren, *From New Bern to Fredericksburg: Captain James Wren's Diary*, ed. John Michael Priest (Shippensburg, PA: White Mane Publishing, Inc., 1990), 93; Jacob Roemer, *Reminiscences of the War of the Rebellion, 1861–1865* (Flushing, NY: Estate of Jacob Roemer, 1897), 98–99. Also see Thomas H. Parker, *History of the 51ˢᵗ Regiment P.V. and V.V.* (Philadelphia, PA: King and Baird, 1869), 262. When Battery A, First Rhode Island Light Artillery, arrived at Falmouth on November 19, Private Thomas Aldrich remembered, "I went down to the [Rappahannock] river myself and had quite a conversation with them [Confederate pickets]. They seemed to be well aware of the change that had been made in commanders." See Thomas M. Aldrich, *The History of Battery A, First Rhode Island Light Artillery, 1861–1865* (Providence, RI: Snow and Farnham, 1904), 156.

118. Marvel, *Burnside*, 168; O'Reilly, *Fredericksburg Campaign*, 50–51.

119. O'Reilly, *Fredericksburg Campaign*, 51; *JCCW*, pt. 1, 671, 674–76.

120. Lincoln is quoted in Rable, *Fredericksburg! Fredericksburg!*, 393; Herman Haupt, *Reminiscences of General Herman Haupt*, ed. Frank Abial Flower (Milwaukee, WI: Wright and Joys, 1901), 177.

121. O'Reilly, *Fredericksburg Campaign*, 51; *JCCW*, pt. 1, 657.

122. Sumner is quoted in O' Reilly, *Fredericksburg Campaign*, 50.

123. *JCCW*, pt. 1, 654, 666; *OR*, ser. I, vol. 21, 774.

124. *JCCW*, pt. 1, 666; O'Reilly, *Fredericksburg Campaign*, 51.

125. Marvel, *Burnside*, 168–69; O'Reilly, *Fredericksburg Campaign*, 51; *JCCW*, pt. 1, 658.

126. *OR*, ser. I, vol. 21, 563, 642–43; U.S. Naval Records Office, *Official Records of the Union and Confederate Navies in the War of the Rebellion*, ser. I, vol. 5, 182–83; O'Reilly, *Fredericksburg Campaign*, 51–52.

127. James Longstreet, "The Battle of Fredericksburg," in *Battles and Leaders of the Civil War*, vol. 3, 72.

128. O'Reilly, *Fredericksburg Campaign*, 52–53; *OR*, ser. I, vol. 21, 64, 87–88; Rable, *Fredericksburg! Fredericksburg!*, 154; Darius N. Couch, "Sumner's 'Right Grand Division,'" in *Battles and Leaders of the Civil War*, vol. 3, 108; Oliver Otis Howard, *Autobiography of Major General Oliver Otis Howard*, vol. 1 (New York: Baker and Taylor Company, 1907), 321.

129. O'Reilly, *Fredericksburg Campaign*, 54, 58–59, 63–67, 70, 72; Harrison, *Fredericksburg Civil War Sites, April 1861–November 1862*, vol. 1, 90–91, 97–99; Harrison, *Fredericksburg Civil War Sites, December 1862–April 1865*, vol. 2, 64–66.

130. O'Reilly, *Fredericksburg Campaign*, 59, 67–69, 76–78; Henry Robinson Berkeley, *Four Years in the Confederate Artillery* (Chapel Hill: University of North Carolina Press, 1961), 36; Hamilton, "An Eyewitness Account of the Battle of Fredericksburg," 7; Catherine S. Crary, *Dear Belle: Letters from a Cadet and Officer to His Sweetheart* (Middletown, CT: Wesleyan University Press, 1965), 173.

131. O'Reilly, *Fredericksburg Campaign*, 78; Rable, *Fredericksburg! Fredericksburg!*, 168; Harrison, *Fredericksburg Civil War Sites*, vol. 2, 56.

132. Modern, in-depth narratives of the street fighting in Fredericksburg on December 11, 1862, include Richard F. Miller and Robert F. Mooney, "Across the River and Into the Streets: The 20th Massachusetts Infantry and the Fight for the Streets in Fredericksburg" in *Blood on the Rappahannock*, especially 115–22; Rable, *Fredericksburg! Fredericksburg!*, especially 168–73; and O'Reilly, *Fredericksburg Campaign*, 79–101.

133. Edward Linden Waitt, comp., *History of the Nineteenth Regiment, Massachusetts Volunteer Infantry, 1861–1865* (Salem, MA: Salem Press, 1906), 167; O'Reilly, *Fredericksburg Campaign*, 83–85; Miller and Mooney, "Across the River," 113–14.

134. O'Reilly, *Fredericksburg Campaign*, 83, 87, 89–91; Letter of Lieutenant Henry C. Ropes to John, December 18, 1862 (typescript courtesy of the Boston Public Library) in Bound Volume #248, Fredericksburg and Spotsylvania National Military Park, National Park Service, Fredericksburg, Virginia.

135. John G.B. Adams, *Reminiscences of the Nineteenth Massachusetts Regiment* (Boston: Wright & Potter, 1899), 50; *History of the Nineteenth Regiment*, 171.

136. O'Reilly, *Fredericksburg Campaign*, 91–93; Letter of Lieutenant Henry C. Ropes to John, December 18, 1862, National Park Service, Fredericksburg, Virginia.

137. Letter of Lieutenant Henry C. Ropes to John, December 18, 1862, National Park Service, Fredericksburg, Virginia; George A. Bruce, *The*

Twentieth Regiment of Massachusetts Volunteer Infantry, 1861–1865 (Boston: Houghton, Mifflin, and Company, 1906), 201–2; O'Reilly, *Fredericksburg Campaign*, 93.

138. *History of the Nineteenth Regiment*, 171; Adams, *Reminiscences*, 50; O'Reilly, *Fredericksburg Campaign*, 93–94.

139. *History of the Nineteenth Regiment*, 172–73; Bruce, *Twentieth Regiment*, 206–7; O'Reilly, *Fredericksburg Campaign*, 85–86.

140. Federal soldier quoted in Harrison, *Fredericksburg Civil War Sites*, vol. 1, 93.

141. Crary, *Dear Belle*, 175–76; Wren, *From New Bern to Fredericksburg*, 97.

142. *OR*, ser. I, vol. 21, 219–20.

143. William Farrar Smith, "Franklin's 'Left Grand Division'" in *Battles and Leaders of the Civil War*, vol. 3, 131, 133; Harrison, *Fredericksburg Civil War Sites*, vol. 2, 77–79; *OR*, ser. I, vol. 21, 64; Marvel, *Burnside*, 176–77, 180; William Marvel, "The Making of a Myth: Ambrose E. Burnside and the Union High Command at Fredericksburg," in *Fredericksburg Campaign: Decision on the Rappahannock*, 10; Snell, *From First to Last*, 211–17; Rable, *Fredericksburg! Fredericksburg!*, 157; O'Reilly, *Fredericksburg Campaign*, 73, 76, 117–18.

144. *OR*, ser. I, vol. 21, 355–56.

145. Marvel, *Burnside*, 180; O'Reilly, *Fredericksburg Campaign*, 118.

146. *OR*, ser. I, vol. 21, 71.

147. *OR*, ser. I, vol. 21, 90.

148. *OR*, ser. I, vol. 21, 90.

CHAPTER 4

149. Longstreet and Jackson are quoted in Robertson, *Stonewall Jackson*, 653–54; O'Reilly, *Fredericksburg Campaign*, 127–28; Harrison, *Fredericksburg Civil War Sites*, vol. 2, 152; and Jeffry D. Wert, *General James Longstreet*, 219.

150. Henry Kyd Douglas, *I Rode With Stonewall* (Chapel Hill: University of North Carolina Press, 1940), 196.

151. J.B. Hood, *Advance and Retreat: Personal Experiences in the United States and Confederate States Armies* (New Orleans, LA: Hood Memorial Fund, 1880), 50; O'Reilly, *Fredericksburg Campaign*, 128; *OR*, ser. I, vol. 21, 570, 622.

152. Harrison, *Fredericksburg Civil War Sites*, vol. 2, 82.

153. Cullum, *Biographical Register*, vol. 2, *1841–1867*, 57; Hal Bridges, *Lee's Maverick General: Daniel Harvey Hill*, ed. Gary W. Gallagher (New York:

McGraw-Hill, 1961; Lincoln: University of Nebraska Press, 1991), 6, 16–17, 23–25.

154. Wert, *General James Longstreet*, 91; Hennessy, *Return to Bull Run*, 61; Bridges, *Lee's Maverick General*, 33; Robertson, *Stonewall Jackson*, 632, 678–79.

155. William T. Poague, *Gunner with Stonewall: Reminiscences of William Thomas Pogue*, ed. Monroe F. Cockrell (Wilmington, NC: Broadfoot Publishing, 1987), 31.

156. Cullum, *Biographical Register*, vol. 2, 189; James I. Robertson Jr., *General A.P. Hill: The Story of a Confederate Warrior* (1987; New York: Vintage Books, 1992), 26–29; William Woods Hassler, *A.P. Hill: Lee's Forgotten General* (1957; Chapel Hill: University of North Carolina Press, 1995), 27.

157. Robertson, *A.P. Hill*, 95–98, 152–54; Wert, *General James Longstreet*, 153–55; *OR*, ser. I, vol. 11, pt. 3, 918–19.

158. Robertson, *A.P. Hill*, 152–54; Robertson, *Stonewall Jackson*, 627–28; and *OR*, ser. I, vol. 19, pt. 2, 643. A.P. Hill is quoted in Robertson, *A.P. Hill*, 157, and Stephen W. Sears, *Chancellorsville* (New York: Houghton Mifflin Company, 1996), 151.

159. Cullum, *Biographical Register*, vol. 1, 674; Osborne, *Jubal*, 14, 16, 23–31; John S. Salmon and Emily J. Salmon, *Franklin County, Virginia, 1786–1986: A Bicentennial History* (Rocky Mount, VA: Franklin County Bicentennial Commission, 1993), 255–57.

160. Osborne, *Jubal*, 130, 228; Robertson, *Stonewall Jackson*, 642.

161. Ezra J. Warner, *Generals in Gray: Lives of Confederate Commanders* (Baton Rogue: Louisiana State University Press, 1959), 297–98.

162. O'Reilly, *Fredericksburg Campaign*, 130; Robertson, *Stonewall Jackson*, 316, 353–54.

163. O'Reilly, *Fredericksburg Campaign*, 128–35; Gregory A. Mertz, "'A Severe Day on the Artillery': Stonewall Jackson's Artillerists and the Defense of the Confederate Right," in *Blood on the Rappahannock*, 71–76; Hassler, *A.P. Hill*, 117–19; Robertson, *A.P. Hill*, 161–68; Robertson, *Stonewall Jackson*, 651–55; Jackson is quoted in Heros von Borcke, *Memoirs of the Confederate War for Independence*, vol. 2 (London, UK: William Blackwood and Sons, 1866), 106, 114–17. O'Reilly has established the fact that the Confederate high command—from division commander A.P. Hill to army commander Robert E. Lee—was aware of the gap on the Confederate right, rendering past scholarship on the culpability concerning the gap, especially on Hill, obsolete. It is clear that the placement of the artillery on Jackson's front and their increased role in that sector stemmed from the difficult terrain that produced the gap.

164. *OR*, ser. I, vol. 21, 71; *JCCW*, pt. 1, 707–8; Smith, "Franklin's 'Left Grand Division,'" *Battles and Leaders of the Civil War*, vol. 3, 133–34; Marvel, "Making of a Myth," in *Fredercksburg Campaign: Decision on the Rappahannock*, 11–14; O'Reilly, *Fredericksburg Campaign*, 135–38.

165. Cullum, *Biographical Register*, vol. 2, 22–23; O'Reilly, *Fredericksburg Campaign*, 112.

166. Cullum, *Biographical Register*, vol. 2, 114–15; O'Reilly, *Fredericksburg Campaign*, 111–12.

167. Cullum, *Biographical Register*, vol. 2, 192–93; Bridges, *Lee's Maverick General*, 23, 113; Alan T. Nolan, *The Iron Brigade*, 2nd ed. (Madison: State Historical Society of Wisconsin, 1961, 1975), 40–41.

168. Cullum, *Biographical Register*, vol. 2, 54–55; O'Reilly, *"Stonewall" Jackson at Fredericksburg*, 22.

169. Cullum, *Biographical Register*, vol. 1, 601–2; Meade, *Life and Letters*, vol. 1, 329, 331–33.

170. O'Reilly, *"Stonewall" Jackson at Fredericksburg*, 22, 34–35; Frank A. O'Reilly, "'Busted Up and Gone to Hell': The Assault of the Pennsylvania Reserves at Fredericksburg," in *The Fredericksburg Campaign: Decision on the Rappahannock*, 2.

171. William Thomas Harbaugh Brooks of Ohio and Albion Parris Howe of Maine were 1841 graduates of West Point. John Newton of Virginia graduated from West Point in 1842. O'Reilly considers Howe to have been "the least cliquish divisional commander in the Sixth Corps, or at least the most independent of its officers." Cullum, *Biographical Register*, vol. 2, 9–10, 34–35, 38–40; O'Reilly, *"Stonewall" Jackson at Fredericksburg*, 21–22; Charles Lanman, *Dictionary of the United States Congress*, 3rd ed. (Washington, D.C.: Government Printing Office, 1866), 279; "Genealogy-Newton of Norfolk," *Virginia Magazine of History and Biography* 30 (1922): 308.

172. Cullum, *Biographical Register*, vol. 2, 425; G.D. Bayard to J.E.B. Stuart, April 4, 1861, J.E.B. Stuart Papers, 1851–1968, Virignia Historical Society, Richmond, Virginia, microfilm reel C621, frame, 754; Samuel J. Bayard, *The Life of George Dashiell Bayard* (New York: G.P. Putnam's Sons, 1874), 12–13, 171–80; O'Reilly, *"Stonewall" Jackson at Fredericksburg*, 22.

173. Bayard, *Life of George Dashiell Bayard*, 206, 261; O'Reilly, *"Stonewall" Jackson at Fredericksburg*, 22; O'Reilly, *Fredericksburg Campaign*, 112; Cullum, *Biographical Register*, vol. 1, 39.

174. O'Reilly, *"Stonewall" Jackson at Fredericksburg*, 23–24; O'Reilly, *Fredericksburg Campaign*, 114–15; *OR*, ser. I, vol. 21, 622.

175. Franklin is quoted in both Snell, *From First to Last*, 220, and Charles S. Wainwright, *A Diary of Battle: The Personal Journals of Colonel Charles S. Wainwright, 1861–1865*, ed. Allan Nevins (New York: Da Capo Press, 1998), 143; O'Reilly, *"Stonewall" Jackson at Fredericksburg*, 35; O'Reilly, *Fredericksburg Campaign*, 138–39.

176. *JCCW*, pt. 1, 691, 698, 715; O'Reilly, *Fredericksburg Campaign*, 140, 152.

177. O'Reilly, *Fredericksburg Campaign*, 139.

178. Cullum, *Biographical Register*, vol. 2, 151; O'Reilly, "'Busted Up and Gone to Hell,'" in *Blood on the Rappahannock*, 10–11; O'Reilly, *"Stonewall" Jackson at Fredericksburg*, 36.

179. *OR*, ser. I, vol. 21, 509, 515, 518; O'Reilly, "'Busted Up and Gone to Hell,'" in *Blood on the Rappahannock*, 10–11; O'Reilly, *"Stonewall" Jackson at Fredericksburg*, 35–40; O'Reilly, *Fredericksburg Campaign*, 139–41.

180. O'Reilly, *Fredericksburg Campaign*, 141; William P. Lloyd, *History of the First Reg't Pennsylvania Reserve Cavalry* (Philadelphia, PA: King and Baird, 1864), 38.

181. Lee is quoted in Wert. William Woods Hassler, *Colonel John Pelham: Lee's Boy Artillerist* (1960; Chapel Hill: University of North Carolina Press, 1995), 142, 145–46; O'Reilly, *"Stonewall" Jackson at Fredericksburg*, 40; Wert, *Cavalryman of the Lost Cause*, 190–91; O'Reilly, *Fredericksburg Campaign*, 143–45.

182. William W. Strong, ed., *History of the 121st Regiment Pennsylvania Volunteers* (Philadelphia, PA: Catholic Standard and Times Press, 1906), 31; *OR*, ser. I, vol. 21, 514–15.

183. Meade and McCandless are quoted in O'Reilly, *"Stonewall" Jackson at Fredericksburg*, 43–45, 51, 63–64; Wert, *Cavalryman of the Lost Cause*, 190–91.

184. *JCCW*, pt. 1, 692; O'Reilly, "'Busted Up and Gone to Hell,'" in *Blood on the Rappahannock*, 13–14; O'Reilly, *"Stonewall" Jackson at Fredericksburg*, 64–65; O'Reilly, *Fredericksburg Campaign*, 166–87; Robert K. Krick, "Maxcy Gregg: Political Extremist and Confederate General," *Civil War History* 19 (1973): 5, 22, also reprinted in Robert K. Krick, *The Smoothbore Volley that Doomed the Confederacy: The Death of Stonewall Jackson and Other Chapters on the Army of Northern Virginia* (Baton Rogue: Louisiana State University Press, 2002), 168–69. Krick's article (and reprinted book chapter) remains the only comprehensive biographical work on Gregg, who was a South Carolina lawyer and a staunch supporter of Southern rights, as well as had eclectic interests in philosophy and astronomy, as evidenced by an impressive personal library and observatory in his home. Krick notes that although Gregg supported a reopening of the international slave trade,

"he opposed the [South Carolina ordinance of secession] on the grounds that it was too heavily concerned with slavery, thus being a dishonor to the memory of those…who had fought the tariff, internal improvements, and the bank."

185. E.M. Woodward, *Our Campaigns or, the Marches, Bivouacs, Battles, Incidents of Camp Life and History of our Regiment During Its Three Years Term of Service* (Philadelphia, PA: John E. Potter, 1865), 236; O'Reilly, *Fredericksburg Campaign*, 180–81.

186. O'Reilly, *Fredericksburg Campaign*, 187–97.

187. *JCCW*, pt. 1, 692–93, 705. O'Reilly, *Fredericksburg Campaign*, 198–99, 215–16.

188. *OR*, ser. I, vol. 21, 66; Jubal A. Early, *Lieutenant General Jubal Anderson Early, C.S.A.: Autobiographical Sketch and Narrative of the War Between the States* (Philadelphia, PA: J.B. Lippincott Company, 1912), 172–75; O'Reilly, *Fredericksburg Campaign*, 203–7.

189. Samuel D. Buck, *With the Old Confeds: Actual Experiences of a Captian in the Line* (Baltimore, MD: H.E. Houck, 1925), 74; O'Reilly, *Fredericksburg Campaign*, 207–12, 221–38.

190. Meade is quoted in O'Reilly, *Fredericksburg Campaign*, 238–44, 355. Bayard, *Life of George Dashiell Bayard*, 273–77; Snell, *From First to Last*, 227.

191. O'Reilly, *Fredericksburg Campaign*, 356–63; George Edward Pickett and La Salle Corbell Pickett, *The Heart of a Soldier: As Revealed in the Intimate Letters of Genl. George E. Picket, C.S.A.* (New York: Seth Moyle, 1913), 65.

192. Standard casualty figures for both sides at Prospect Hill are generally rounded to five thousand (Federal) and four thousand (Confederate). *OR*, ser. I, vol. 21, 129–42, 558–62, 573, 610, 623, 629, 635, 640, 667. Also see O'Reilly, *"Stonewall" Jackson at Fredericksburg*, 196.

Chapter 5

193. *JCCW*, pt. 1, 657; Couch, "Sumner's Right Grand Division," 110.

194. *OR*, ser. I, vol. 21, 219; O'Reilly, *Fredericksburg Campaign*, 246–47; Cullum, *Biographical Register*, vol. 1, 148.

195. *OR*, ser. I, vol. 21, 219, 311; Cullum, *Biographical Register*, vol. 2, 184–85.

196. *OR*, ser. I, vol. 21, 222, 263; Cullum, *Biographical Register*, vol. 1, 531–32, vol. 2, 108–9, 369–70; Robertson, *Stonewall Jackson*, 100–109; Couch, "Sumner's Right Grand Division," 110–11; Howard, *Autobiography*, vol. 1, 53, 327; John A. Carpenter, *Sword and Olive Branch: Oliver Otis Howard*

(Bronx, NY: Fordham University Press, 1999), 9; Thomas, *Bold Dragoon*, 25, 30; O'Reilly, *Fredericksburg Campaign*, 247.

197. William Miller Owen, *In Camp and Battle with the Washington Artillery Battalion* (Boston: Ticknor and Company, 1885), 185–86; O'Reilly, *Fredericksburg Campaign*, 105–6, 249, 254; Harrison, *Fredericksburg Civil War Sites, December 1862–April 1865*, vol. 2, 149, 160–61; Alexander, *Fighting for the Confederacy*, 167–69.

198. O'Reilly, *Fredericksburg Campaign*, 254; Owen, *In Camp and Battle*, 184, 186.

199. Longstreet, "The Battle of Fredericksburg," in *Battles and Leaders*, vol. 3, 79; Alexander, *Fighting for the Confederacy*, 169.

200. Lafayette McLaws, *A Soldier's General: The Civil War Letters of Major General Lafayette McLaws*, ed. John C. Oeffinger (Chapel Hill: University of North Carolina Press, 2002), 1–23; Cullum, *Biographical Register*, vol. 2, 67; G. Moxley Sorrell, *Recollections of a Confederate Staff Officer* (New York: Neale Publishing Company, 1905), 135; Wert, *General James Longstreet*, 209.

201. Cullum, *Biographical Register*, vol. 2, 63; C. Irvine Walker, *The Life of Lieutenant General Richard Heron Anderson of the Confederate States Army* (Charleston, SC: Art Publishing Company, 1917), 23; Sorrell, *Recollections of a Confederate Staff Officer*, 136; Wert, *General James Longstreet*, 209.

202. Hood, *Advance and Retreat*, 16, 50; Cullum, *Biographical Register*, vol. 2, 362–63; Sorrell, *Recollections of a Confederate Staff Officer*, 135–36.

203. Cullum, *Biographical Register*, vol. 2, 179–80; Sorrell, *Recollections of a Confederate Staff Officer*, 54 136; Edward G. Longacre, *Leader of the Charge: A Biography of General George E. Pickett* (Shippensburg, PA: White Mane Publishing Company, 1995), 23; Wert, *General James Longstreet*, 45, 210.

204. Cullum, *Biographical Register*, vol. 2, 263–64; Wert, *General James Longstreet*, 210.

205. O'Reilly, *Fredericksburg Campaign*, 247–55; Franklin Sawyer, *A Military History of the 8th Regiment Ohio Volunteer Infantry* (Cleveland, OH: Fairbanks and Company, 1881), 93–95; William P. Seville, *History of the First Regiment, Delaware Volunteers* (Wilmington: Historical Society of Delaware, 1884), 57.

206. O'Reilly, *Fredericksburg Campaign*, 256–57; Sawyer, *Military History*, 96; Frederick H.L. Hitchcock, *War From the Inside* (Philadelphia, PA: J.B. Lippincott Company, 1904), 121.

207. O'Reilly, *Fredericksburg Campaign*, 258–59; Robert Ransom, "Ransom's Division at Fredericksburg," in *Battles and Leaders*, vol. 3, 94.

208. Couch, "Sumner's 'Right Grand Division,'" in *Battles and Leaders*, vol. 3, 113; O'Reilly, *Fredericksburg Campaign*, 294–96.

209. O'Reilly, *Fredericksburg Campaign*, 296–97; Harrison, *Fredericksburg Civil War Sites, December 1862–April 1865*, vol. 2, 129–30. For the historical controversy surrounding the circumstances of Cobb's wounding, see David L. Preston, "'The Glorious Light Went Out Forever': The Death of Brigadier General Thomas R.R. Cobb," in *Blood on the Rappahannock*, 28–46. Cobb, the younger brother of former U.S. Speaker of the House and former Georgia governor Howell Cobb, was an attorney, author and staunch advocate for Southern secession and the institution of slavery. The only full-length biography on Cobb remains William B. McCash, *Thomas R.R. Cobb (1823–1862): The Making of a Southern Nationalist* (Macon, GA: Mercer University Press, 1983, 2004).

210. O'Reilly, *Fredericksburg Campaign*, 293–323; Gilbert Frederick, *The Story of a Regiment* (Chicago, IL: Fifty-Seventh Veteran Association, 1895), 121; Winthrop D. Sheldon, *"The Twenty-Seventh": A Regimental History* (New Haven, CT: Morris and Benham, 1866), 25–28; William McCarter and Kevin E. O'Brien, "'The Breath of Hell's Door': Private William McCarter and the Irish Brigade at Fredericksburg," in *Blood on the Rappahannock*, 51, 59–60; D.P. Conyngham, *The Irish Brigade and Its Campaigns* (New York: William McSorely and Company, 1867), 343; *OR*, ser. I, vol. 21, 233–34.

211. D. Augustus Dickert, *History of Kershaw's Brigade* (Newberry, SC: Elbert H. Hall Company, 1899), 185; *OR*, ser. I, vol. 21, 589.

212. Couch, "Sumner's 'Right Grand' Division," in *Battles and Leaders*, vol. 3, 113; Howard, *Autobiography*, vol. 1, 342–43; Cullum, *Biographical Register*, vol. 2, 159–60; Leander W. Cogswell, *A History of the Eleventh New Hampshire* (Concord, NH: Republican Press Association, 1891), 53–54; Walcott, *History of the Twenty-first Massachusetts Volunteers*, 241; Parker, *History of the 51st*, 271, 273; Edward O. Lord, ed., *History of the Ninth Regiment New Hampshire Volunteers in the War of the Rebellion* (Concord, NH: Republican Press Association, 1895), 196–97; *History of the Twelfth Regiment Rhode Island Volunteers in the Civil War, 1862–1863*, ed. Committee of the Survivors (Providence RI: Snow and Farnham, 1904), 274; Lyman Jackman, *History of the Sixth New Hampshire Regiment in the War for the Union* (Concord NH: Republican Press Association, 1891), 127–28; Wren, *From New Bern to Fredericksburg*, 96; O'Reilly, *Fredericksburg Campaign*, 324–54.

213. O'Reilly, *Fredericksburg Campaign*, 275, 322, 351.

214. Ibid., 363, 376–81, 388; *OR*, ser. I, vol. 21, 397, 399; Donaldson, *Inside the Army of the Potomac*, 184; Eugene Arus Nash, *Forty-Fourth Regiment New York Volunteer Infantry in the Civil War, 1861–1865* (Chicago, IL: R.R. Donnelley and Sons Company, 1911), 115.

215. O'Reilly, *Fredericksburg Campaign*, 355–56, 389; Couch, "Sumner's Right Grand Division," 113–15.

216. Alexander, *Fighting for the Confederacy*, 177–79; John H. Rhodes, *The History of Battery B, First Regiment Rhode Island Light Artillery* (Providence, RI: Snow and Farnham, 1894), 140; O'Reilly, *Fredericksburg Campaign*, 389–90, 397, 400–401.

217. *OR*, ser. I, vol. 21, 430; Couch, "Sumner's 'Right Grand' Division," in *Battles and Leaders*, vol. 3, 114; Carol Reardon, "The Forlorn Hope: Brigadier General Andrew A. Humphreys's Pennsylvania Division at Fredericksburg," in *Fredericksburg Campaign: Decision on the Rappahannock*, 90–98; O'Reilly, *Fredericksburg Campaign*, 406–12.

218. Rush C. Hawkins, "Why Burnside Did Not Renew the Attack at Fredericksburg," *Battles and Leaders*, vol. 3, 127; *JCCW*, pt. 1, 668. Standard casualty figures for both sides at Marye's Heights are generally rounded to 8,000 (Federal) and 1,500 (Confederate). *OR*, ser. I, vol. 21, 129–42, 558–62, 573, 610, 623, 629, 635, 640, 667.

CHAPTER 6

219. Lee is quoted in Thomas, *Robert E. Lee*, 271; Augustus Buell, *The Cannoneer: Recollections of Service in the Army of the Potomac* (Washington, D.C.: National Tribune, 1890), 44. Standard casualty figures for both sides in the Battle of Fredericksburg generally round to 12,500 (Federal) and 5,000 (Confederate); *OR*, ser. I, vol. 21, 129–42, 558–62, 573, 610, 623, 629, 635, 640, 667.

220. "Battle of Fredericksburg," *Fredericksburg (VA) Free Lance*, December 24, 1910, in Bound Volume #139, FRSP; "Our Army Correspondence," *Mobile (AL) Register and Advertiser*, December 30, 1862, Staff Historian Files, FRSP; Sanford Branch Letter, December 19, 1862, in Bound Volume #26, FRSP; Dickert, *History of Kershaw's Brigade*, 193, 196–97.

221. John Haley, *The Rebel Yell and Yankee Hurrah: The Civil War Journal of a Maine Volunteer*, ed. Ruth L. Siliker (Camden, ME: Down East Books, 1987), 59; Rush C. Hawkins, "Why Burnside Did Not Renew the Attack," *Battles and Leaders*, vol. 3, 127; Joshua L. Chamberlain, "My Story of Fredericksburg," *Cosmopolitan Magazine* 54 (January 1913): 154.

222. O'Reilly, *Fredericksburg Campaign*, 439.

223. Ibid., 431–32, 436; *OR*, ser. I, vol. 21, 224; Hawkins, "Why Burnside Did Not Renew the Attack," *Battles and Leaders*, vol. 3, 127; Couch,

"Sumner's Right Grand Division," *Battles and Leaders*, vol. 3, 117–18; Smith, "Franklin's 'Left Grand Division,'" *Battles and Leaders*, vol. 3, 137–38.

224. O'Reilly, *Fredericksburg Campaign*, 445–50; John H. Worsham, *One of Jackson's Foot Cavalry* (New York: Neale Publishing Company, 1912), 154.

225. Franklin L. Riley, *Grandfather's Journal: Company B, Sixteenth Mississippi Infantry Volunteers, Harris' Brigade, Mahone's Division, Hill's Corps, A.N.V., May 27, 1861–July 15, 1865*, ed. Austin C. Dobbins (Dayton, OH: Morningside, 1988), 114–15; Sorrell, *Recollections of a Confederate Staff Officer*, 145–46.

226. O'Reilly, *Fredericksburg Campaign*, 460; Marvel, *Burnside*, 202–8; Snell, *From First to Last*, 234–36; A.W. Greene, "Morale, Maneuver, and Mud: The Army of the Potomac, December 16, 1862–January 26, 1863," in *Fredericksburg Campaign: Decision on the Rappahannock*, 179–80; "From the Army of the Potomac: An Important Letter from Gen. Burnside," *New York Times*, December 23, 1862.

227. *JCCW*, pt. 1, 716–17; Greene, "Morale, Maneuver, and Mud," 180–81; O'Reilly, *Fredericksburg Campaign*, 464–68; Thomas, *Bold Dragoon*, 195–200; Wert, *Cavalryman of the Lost Cause*, 195–98.

228. Greene, "Morale, Maneuver, and Mud," 180–86; O'Reilly, *Fredericksburg Campaign*, 469–71; Snell, *From First to Last*, 236–37; *JCCW*, pt. 1, 717, 730–46.

229. *JCCW*, pt. 1, 717–19; Greene, "Morale, Maneuver, and Mud," 186–89; O'Reilly, *Fredericksburg Campaign*, 471–72.

230. *OR*, ser. I, vol. 21, 96, 752–55; *JCCW*, pt. 1, 719; Greene, "Morale, Maneuver, and Mud," 195–206; O'Reilly, *Fredericksburg Campaign*, 475–89.

231. *OR*, ser. I, vol. 21, 998–99, 1,004–5; *JCCW*, pt. 1, 719–21.

232. *OR*, ser. I, vol. 21, 1005.

Conclusion

233. Thomas, *Robert E. Lee*, 273; *OR*, ser. I, vol. 21, 549–50.

234. *OR*, ser. I, vol. 21, 67–68.

235. "Final Emancipation Proclamation," *Abraham Lincoln: Speeches and Writings*, 424–25. Both Douglass and the *Richmomd Daily Dispatch* editorial are quoted in Rable, *Fredericksburg! Fredericksburg!*, 375–76, 378.

236. Meade, *Life and Letters*, vol. 1, 349. Lincoln is quoted in Rable, *Fredericksburg! Fredericksburg!*, 42.

237. *OR*, ser. I, vol. 25, 4; D.G. Crotty, *Four Years Campaigning in the Army of the Potomac* (Grand Rapids, MI: Dygert Brothers and Company, 1874), 81.

About the Author

Jim Bryant is a former associate professor of history at Shenandoah University in Winchester, Virginia, where he served five years as the department chair and one year as executive director of Shenandoah University's History and Tourism Center. He was also a historian with the National Park Service, spending nine years with the Fredericksburg and Spotsylvania National Military Park that encompasses the Fredericksburg Battlefield. He lives currently in Stephens City, Virginia, with his wife Amy and sons Jack and Trip.

Visit us at
www.historypress.net